MW00425849

How to MAKE It in a World that WASN'T MADE for You

LARRY H. JEMISON JR.

How to Make It in a World that Wasn't Made for You

Copyright © 2008 Larry H. Jemison Jr. All rights
reserved. No part of this book may be reproduced or
retransmitted in any form or by any means without
the written permission of the publisher.

Published by Wheatmark™
610 East Delano Street, Suite 104
Tucson, Arizona 85705 U.S.A.
www.wheatmark.com

ISBN: 978-1-58736-919-3
LCCN: 2007933243

ACKNOWLEDGEMENTS

The inspiration for this book comes from my family, Larry Sr. (Big Jem), Elizabeth (The Twig), Ledra, Cousin George IV, and my grandparents, who have all been exceptional role models on my journey to success. Outsiders often viewed my family as the real-life Cosbys. These individuals have never seen a bad day, and if they have, they let very few people notice it. I think they have bought into the fact that we all have two choices: be the victor and enjoy each day, or be the victim and cry about how life has treated us poorly.

They choose victory, they choose to win, and they choose to live each day to the fullest.

They attack issues head-on so that a small problem never has a chance to snowball into something much larger. Simply following in their footsteps and abiding by their guidance has made it easy for me to become a man—a real man, a dependable man, who is accountable for both his successes and his failures. I also have to acknowledge my sixth grade teacher, Mrs. Valerie Brown. She demonstrated to me that success could be my only option if I surrounded myself with the right people. She also made it clear that I would need to make wise decisions, decisions that I could either prosper from or have the ability to correct if I made the wrong choice.

As long as we make decisions that we can recover from if they are not the correct choices, then we give ourselves another chance to succeed. It is safe to say that I associate with the right people and have been making wise choices ever since. To my family, and Mrs. Valerie Brown, thank you all.

DEDICATION

After I finished writing this book, a young man enrolled at Tuskegee University was murdered in the streets of Tuskegee, Alabama. Many described him as a kind-hearted, intelligent, and caring individual who was on the path to greatness. He was well-mannered, full of energy, and heavily into mentoring and community service. He seemed to be the kind of person that any parent would be proud of.

I want you to know that I never met this young man, but his spirit lives within me. As a third-generation Tuskegee graduate, I feel a deep bond to the university and the city alike. Though the Tuskegee University student is no longer with us, I know that I must continue to inspire the community to do what they can to stop these types of incidents, which are senseless. Who gave anyone permission to take another man's life? How bad could life have been for the two teenagers charged with killing this young man? Just as the victim's father said, "The greatest tragedy is that three young people's lives have now been destroyed by this."

The poor short-term decisions made by these teens will have lifelong effects on all involved. These are decisions one does not simply correct or prosper from. These are the decisions that we all need to avoid. Children make these poor decisions on a daily basis, and without intervention they will continue to make poor decisions and assume that they are acceptable.

To the surviving parents, I want you to know that you are not alone in your struggle. I think of your son often, knowing that this was not his ultimate destiny. I believe that he is doing God's work at this time and looking down over us all saying, "I sure hope one day they can get it right." I write this book in remembrance of your son, Canon Christopher Jones II.

CONTENTS

Introduction 1

1. Life Is Not Fair...11

2. Display Your Talents; Then Toot Your Horn ..31

3. Believe, Create, and then Go Get It! 45

4. 100 Percent of Success Is Attitude 57

5. Motivation and Politics 79

6. True Leadership in Society 93

7. The Power of Relationships.............................121

8. Education Is the Key..135

9. Get Excited; It's Your Only Option 145

Conclusion 159

About the Author..163

I couldn't wait for success,
so I went ahead without it.
                    —Jonathan Winters

INTRODUCTION

This book is one of the great ones, one of those books that makes you run out and tell everyone they need to read it. It is the type of masterpiece that makes scholars wonder what exactly the author meant when he said, "Life is all the experiences in the world that either you or someone else can remember."

Let's make a pact before you read another word: you will take this book to at least three high schools in your town and tell the guidance counselor that it should be required reading before a student can graduate or a teacher can teach. Then, take it to your job; tell everyone in the office that you hold the key to his or her success. As the strange looks come across their faces, ask them, "How important is your success to you?" Then say, "I can assure your success for less than the price of dinner and a movie." Next, slap the book on the desk, and say, "Read this, and you and your families' lives will never be the same. Give a slight smile, and then say, "You don't have to thank me now, but you can get me that gift certificate for the dinner and the movie!"

Okay, that may be a bit much, and I may be a little off, but I suffer so you don't have to. I may be facetious at times, but researchers say there is a thin line between brilliant and totally whacked out. When left with the option, I say I'm the first: brilliant.

On a more serious note, this is a great book because the surprise ending is given to you on the first page. All you have to do is read the first page, and then put the book down. At that point you will understand my strategy of how to make it in a world that wasn't made for you. You will understand what it takes to be successful. Yeah, right, if only it was that simple, but I am going to provide you a solid foundation for success, because you're worth it. Many other books make life seem so easy, as if there is some secret, magic formula, or cheat code; if you have it, you will be successful, rich, or incredibly blessed, and life will be grand.

I'm here to tell you that life is not like that, and

neither are there cheat codes to access free men or additional plays. This is not PlayStation, and if it were, the children would be teaching the adults, although many days it seems like this is the reality we live in anyway, where parental leadership is very much absent. We will talk more on parental leadership later, but for now let's keep going.

The real message here is that there are a number of books that teach you how to be successful and brag about how wealthy or powerful the author is. Then, at some point, you find out that the author was born into money, inherited money, or had a lucky break along the way. That is not the success I am speaking of. This book is about applying the tools and principles of success, so you and everyone you know has an adequate amount of opportunities to succeed.

This book is intended for the masses but positioned especially for you. It will benefit students, teachers, parents, entrepreneurs, corporate citizens, athletes, and entertainers alike. For those of us categorized as underachievers and maybe lazy, this resource will be particularly invaluable. The following chapters contain the ingredients that will make you believe, make you passionate, and make you successful. We will start from the beginning, and as you read deeper and further, the lessons will all come together. *Just as sure as the sun will rise tomorrow, so will you!*

Regarding success, I would love to own thirty-five commercial real estate investments across the country and do another ten to twenty deals a year worldwide. I think we would all love to be in that situation, but unfortunately I was not born into wealth, do not have unlimited resources, and am forced to work hard every day if I want to succeed. The scars I have came from battling life's obstacles, not from someone simply giving me things. The journey to success is not an easy one, and it will not be easy for you. We must all wake up with a mission in mind to be better than we were yesterday. Then, when the opportunity to succeed presents itself, we must be ready to seize it, instead of waiting for someone to hand it to us.

Each experience in life has made me that much stronger, that much more confident, so that I can fight toward success every day. This story is about the real, common person's guide to success. Traditional methods are highlighted and elaborated on so that everyone who reads this book can become successful beyond their wildest dreams.

Keep in mind that when I say "successful," I do not always equate success with financial prosperity. Success can be having a great family bond; receiving numerous accolades at work, school, or church; earning the respect of friends; and overall becoming a great person, without losing sight of financial bliss. With this said, I hope while you are

4

achieving all of this success you remain excited about making money. At the end of the day, that is why we work, create companies, and constantly strive for success. Let's get to it; let's start our journey for success. *Today is the tomorrow that we spoke about yesterday, and we can no longer procrastinate.*

The Beginning of My Success

I knew ever since I was a little boy that I would be successful. I had my own definition of success from day one. In my mind anyone who had a nice car and a big house was successful. Life was just that simple. I was six years old, playing Bingo every day with my older sister and cousin. Bingo was not the well-known game of numbers; it was what we played when we imagined having the nice cars we saw drive by while running errands with my parents.

As we rode around the city of Memphis we saw these nice cars, and the first person to say "Bingo" and the name of the car got the car, at least in pretend mode. So my sister would say, "Bingo that Mercedes Benz," it would become hers, and nobody else could lay claim to it. You had to be quick on your toes so that you were able to Bingo the best cars. We took this game seriously, and it was not uncommon for one of us to say something like, "Man, that sure was a nice Porsche that I got today," and everyone would think back to the car you had scored earlier that day before anyone else could.

It was not so much the cars but what the cars symbolized that captured our imagination. The fancy cars and the big homes gave us a reason to try harder, to do better. They were our motivation for excellence even at an early age. I remember talking to my father one day and saying, "Dad, one day I'm going to be rich." He responded and said, "I know, Son, I know." My parents believed in us and felt that we would be successful in all that we attempted as long as we envisioned our success, believed in our success, and worked hard for it. After the past few decades, I can tell you my dad was right.

Another thing I knew growing up was that I was a hustler. Not in the illegal sense or that I would treat someone poorly to get what I wanted, but more in the sense that I would do what it took to obtain my desired results. I was a strategist and always planned my every step so I could obtain what I wanted. I was always willing to do my research, to prepare my proposal, to present my offerings and negotiate, and then request exactly what I desired. In business this closely mirrors what is known as the sales process.

I remember my first business deal. I was five years old when we took a family trip to Houston, Texas, to visit my grandparents. It always seemed like the worst trip, because I had to leave all my friends back home, no other kids were in my grandparents' neighborhood, and as the youngest grandchild I felt like the other children had more liberties than I had.

My uncle, who lived across the street from my grandparents, came to us with a proposal. He said that he was building a greenhouse to protect and nurture his prized plants and would pay us (the grand kids) a penny per brick if we helped him lay the foundation. Well, even at five years old, I knew a penny did not go far, especially in the summer heat of Texas, trying to place bricks that weighed four to five pounds apiece.

I followed behind the other children and started laying bricks, which was manual labor at its finest. About an hour into the job, I started thinking to myself that this job was for the birds and we were being underpaid. I took my complaints to my uncle and said, "Hey, look, we need to make more money; it's hot out here; these bricks are heavy; plus, you are not even keeping track of the bricks we are laying, so you don't know what the actual payment amount is." My uncle looked at me with a dazed look, almost as if to say, who are you at five years old to complain about the job and the low wages?

He then proceeded to tell me to get back to work, or he was going to fire me. I said, "Well, fire me then, because this is no fun anyway." My uncle, not wanting to lose one of his laborers, tried to bribe me. He said if I didn't work I wouldn't have the money I needed to go to AstroWorld (a large amusement park in Houston) the next day with the rest of the kids. I said, "Well how much does it cost?" My uncle said it was ten dollars for small kids. I went to my sister and asked how many bricks I had to place to make ten dollars. She smiled and said, "A thousand."

I knew I would never lay that many bricks, as I was tired and bored after the first hour. I immediately walked across the street to my grandmother Grandearie's house, where my dad was. My dad did not like going on these trips because he got bored easily as well. We really just went so that we could spend time with the grandparents and keep my mother happy.

As I walked in the house, my dad was on the couch watching the old TV that got really poor reception because Booze (my grandfather) tried so hard to fix the problems himself, rather than obtaining a professional. That was his thing; he loved to tinker with everything, even if it wasn't broken. My dad's face lit up as I entered the room, because now he had someone to talk to. I said, "Dad, can I have fifteen dollars?" He said, "Well, maybe; what do you need fifteen dollars for?"

I said, "Because all the kids are going to AstroWorld tomorrow, and it costs ten dollars to
get in, but I figure I will have to eat too, so I need
a little extra." My dad said, "Okay, Son, don't
worry about it; I'll make sure you go and that
you get something to eat."

"Really?" I asked.

"Sure, no problem," my dad answered.

"Thanks, Dad, you're the best," I told him.

I walked back across the street to my uncle's
house and told him I quit. I said, "This job does
not pay enough for the work that is involved,
and I can make more than this sitting over there
at Grandma's house watching TV." My uncle
said, "Fine, but don't come back over here asking
for your job back." I immediately turned around,
walked back across the street, and started watching TV with my dad. It was at that point that I
knew I would be a businessman. It was the art of
negotiation, sense of hustle, and thrill of victory
that made me feel good about what I had just
done.

I had successfully negotiated a better wage
for far less work in better working conditions,
even though my dad probably would have paid
for me to go to AstroWorld anyway. After that
experience I never looked back, and now I understand that *everything is negotiable*. That's one
of the first rules of success, and it should be com-

bined with the other lessons of this book. Keep reading as we begin to build your foundation for success.

In three words I can sum up everything
I've learned about life: It goes on.
— Robert Frost

ONE

Life Is Not Fair

This may be one of the most important chapters you will ever read. It pertains to your motivation, determination, competitive spirit, and overall success. Once you grasp the title of this chapter, you will have already begun to achieve greatness. You will be one step closer to conquering your future. Life is never fair to anyone, and successful people have accepted this as fact. Some were born into royalty and wealth, some into poverty and slavery, some drug addicted, some with long legs, and some with no legs.

The fact remains that everybody has his or her own challenges to face. No one person is exempt from hardship. There has never been an imaginary contract signed at birth stating life would be simple. The hardships and scars remind us of where we have been and what we have been through.

We have all had that special love interest who chose to be with someone else or got cut from the team when we felt we were better than the next person. What about getting skipped over for a promotion at work that you thought was yours for sure?

It just does not seem fair, does it? That is because it is not. Life is not fair. Now that you know this, you should accomplish more in a shorter time period with a lot less whining. Learn how to play the game. If you get skipped over, or your number is not called, go back to the drawing board, find out what you could have done differently, and then try again.

Many times, the reason you were not chosen had nothing to do with your performance; rather, it is often because the other candidate was a better fit for the position. Marcus Bailey, CEO of an Atlanta-based recruitment firm, says that employee turnover cost the U.S. economy $420 billion in 2004.[1] With numbers as staggering as these, companies are doing more and more to hire the right candidate the first time. This means that the hiring decision may be based on much more than you are

1   Marcus Bailey, "Fitting Right In, Using assessment to find the right employee," *Black Enterprise Magazine*, August 2006, 78.

able to recognize, given your lack of information about the selection process.

Sharon Hall, who represents another Atlanta-based firm, says that "A person's ability to perform well in a job can be confirmed with the resume and the interview. However, the likelihood of success can sometimes be better projected from the psychological assessment."[2] This further suggests that companies are evaluating many different factors before making a decision, and many times you may not like the outcome or feel that it was fair. If you are not the chosen one, don't complain; sharpen your skills, and continue on; it may just be preparation for what is to come. Was it fair? Who knows? Life is not fair; you win some and you lose some.

I have had many experiences during my twelve-year business career where I wondered if I was getting the fair end of the deal. After nine months of working in sales, my goal attainment had risen from 85 percent to 117 percent — a stretch that was almost impossible. Goal attainment is the amount of revenue you obtain in comparison to the amount of revenue the company has set for you to obtain. If the company says you have to bring in one million dollars of new business per quarter and you bring in exactly one million dollars, then you have hit 100 percent goal attainment. In this example,

2   Sharon Hall, "Fitting Right In, Using assessment to find the right employee," Black Enterprise Magazine, August 2006, 78.

anything above one million puts you over 100 percent, and anything below puts you under.

In a very short time I was blowing away my goal, and I was on track to receive a healthy bonus check. Just as payouts were about to happen, my manager moved me to another territory. This new territory was performing at 78 percent goal attainment, leaving me with a payout that was significantly smaller than what I stood to receive before the transition. I could not believe this was happening after all the hard work I had applied to nurture and grow the first territory.

Why would my manager do this to me knowing that I had worked so hard to earn my bonus? Some said race was involved, while others said it was because I was new and they did not want the new guy outshining the veterans. Instead of earning my $8,000 check, I was getting a $3,000 check at the new territory, while the person who replaced me did nothing and stood to receive my $8,000 bonus.

I chose to dismiss race because I have to be accountable for both my success and my failures, and if something or someone is impeding my results, then I have to find an alternative way to obtain my success. If someone or something is prohibiting you from reaching your goals, you will need to find an alternative solution as well. You will need to realize that failure is short-term and you will not give up until you succeed. The question was, now that I felt shafted, what were my options?

I could repeatedly alert my manager and tell him how disappointed I was, and then report the incident to Human Resources and risk corporate backlash and retaliation from my manager for reporting the offense. I could take my skills to another company where they may be valued more. Or lastly, I could document the incident and keep working to the best of my ability, hoping someone would eventually help my cause.

I chose the latter. I documented everything and continued on with the company, understanding that life is not fair. It was not the easiest thing in the world to do, but at some point we have to realize that life is not fair, and neither should we expect it to be. Oftentimes this is a blessing in disguise.

After working another couple years, my talent was finally recognized. I nurtured the new territory into a winner. My manager was promoted to another position, and the manager who replaced him was excited about my success. I eventually grew the territory to 127 percent goal attainment and received multiple bonus payouts that were much higher than what I would have received in the old area. Losing out on that other bonus check could have driven me crazy had I let it, but I knew that life was not fair, and neither did I expect it to be. *It comes down to you managing the situation and not allowing the situation to manage you.*

You must understand this, and the sooner you do, the sooner your success will come. In life you should take the stance that no one owes you anything. This will spare you a lot of pain along the way. Stand up and be accountable for your success and your failure while realizing that life is not fair. Sometimes we need to change the way we view our problems so we can attack them in the most appropriate manner.

Changing one's life is the only way to conquer life's changes. The more we change the way we see things, the more the things we see will change. Knowing that I was being forced to change in my corporate sales role, I had to really analyze the situation so that I could adjust and make the best decision.

Corporate America may seem like a great world, and for many it is. You work hard for the company, so on the flip side, they reward you with a salary that allows you to comfortably pay your bills month after month. For many, this is the way it is for thirty years without fail. For others, this is not the case, and they are only one ineffective manager away from being without a job.

These corporate jobs, which years ago many kept until retirement, are fading fast, and nothing is ever promised, so never get too comfortable. According to Spencer Stuart, a worldwide executive search firm, the average tenure of a chief executive officer lasts just fifty-four months. The average tenure of a chief marketing officer at *Fortune* companies is even shorter, with tenure averaging a mere twenty-three months.[3] I know you may not be a CEO, but this suggests you should always have a Plan B, including maintaining valuable networks, keeping an updated resume, and saving as much money as you can, so in the event that you lose your job, you are prepared to pack your things and move on. Experts say you should have at least four to twelve months of your monthly expenses saved. For those who have trouble saving, it may be a good idea to meet with a financial planner or your banking manager to see if there is a program to assist you in your savings goals. If we are to truly be successful, we must be prepared when the worst of times hit. As the saying goes, *the best time to prepare for war is during a time of peace.* Business is never fair, and neither is life. You just have to prepare yourself so that you are ready for whatever comes your way.

Knowing that life is not fair, it is always a good idea to document everything. This has become much easier with the invention of the copy machine and email. Your boss will often create a file

3   http://recruitingtrends.com/online/news/308-1.html, Corporate America's Most Perilous Job.

on how well or how poorly you perform. This is standard procedure, but what should also be standard is that *you too should create a file for your records*. When the time comes for you to prove your case, it is much more credible when you have documents and dates that support your claims. At your evaluation, you want to be able to answer with "It says that I do not work well with the community, but what about on June 22, when I chaired the Feed the Homeless Day?" It is hard for anyone to dispute this type of well-documented information.

The moral is that life is not fair, and neither should we expect it to be. By recognizing this principle you can set strategic goals for yourself, obtain these goals, and continue to progress. By accepting this, you are three steps ahead of your competition, who think life owes them something and that success should just come to them.

Realizing that life is not fair or predictable, you must have a solid understanding of who you are. Knowledge of self is the equalizer, the balance that makes life's problems easier to manage. There will be many things in life that you are unsure of, but know who you are, and that will be one thing you can be sure of. This knowledge will allow you to realize what things propel you to be great or in what situations you thrive. A guy who can only hit the fastball cannot be mad when he is thrown a curve. You must prepare ahead of time, so that no matter what comes at you, you are prepared.

You must understand your strengths and your weaknesses, and then improve upon both. When life throws you that curve ball, you have to be ready for it, and if you are not, you need to have the processes in place so you can push the pause button, reflect back on your preparation, make the adjustment, and then when you press pause again, you are ready to knock it out of the park.

There is always someone who is better looking, maybe better dressed, has higher scores, or has access to more than you, but since life is not fair, you have to find an alternative way to display your value. Once this value proposition is displayed, others will want to associate with you or do business with you, and that may be the foot in the door that you have been dreaming about. Above I mentioned race and was quick to dismiss the theory that my territory realignment had anything to do with it. But the fact is that race could have been the sole reason for the transition.

But for me to accept it as such could have made me angry and could have negatively affected my thoughts and allowed for the circumstances to overpower me. I could not allow my boss's decision to alter my controlled state, which might have ruined my judgment and made me act erratically. On top of this, I understand the title of this chapter.

Life is not fair, so don't stop, don't falter, and don't show fear. You are here to claim your success, so you should always be looking at how you can succeed, not for the reasons why you did not.

As for the young woman who inherited my commission check, we are still friends. Sometimes we even laugh at how the whole situation played out. She knew she walked into a gold mine at my expense, but she also knew she would be expected to keep those numbers above 100 percent, and as soon as they fell, people would be looking for her to be accountable for the decrease. And even though I did not receive the check, I did earn the respect of many individuals for my character and the way I handled the situation. One day one of my old teammates may own his or her own company or have a high-ranking position in a company. At that point he or she may say, "He was not treated fairly, but he definitely has the skills we need to assist us in growing. Let's give him a call and hire him for a training session." I would have sacrificed $8,000 only to make potentially far more based on my character and skill sets.

Actually, after getting over the initial shock of losing the commission check, it really was not that bad. My boss's style made me a stronger, better, more results-driven businessman. On top of this, the territory switch actually put me in a position to earn commission checks double the size of the

one I lost. It took a little work, but I was able to ma-
neuver the new territory in a way so that I would
be rewarded for my efforts, compensated for my
new results, and later promoted for my diligence.
In this situation, just as in most, life was not fair,
but lucky for me, I was not expecting it to be.

Respecting Differences and Overcoming Obstacles

One area in which life is especially not fair is that
of differences between people. Areas like race,
which we have touched on, gender, and nationality are often used to discriminate against others.
I have found that despite a person's race, gender,
or nationality most people want to be kind, pro-
ductive citizens. The media often shows individuals of different groups as uneducated, dishonest,
or cruel, and this helps to support stereotypes that
people formulate about each other. Do not fall for
this subliminal brainwashing, and do your best to
learn and understand from as many people and as
many cultures as possible. Do not let race or racism
cause you to miss out on some of the best experiences life has to offer.

Given a chance, we can all learn from each other, do business with each other, and enjoy life to
the fullest, with few resentments or regrets. Open
your mind, and be a friend to as many people as
possible from as many places as possible. The business term for this is *networking*. You will have just

opened the doors to many more opportunities, doors which ordinarily would have been closed. Understand that life is not fair, but that does not mean you should not be. To succeed in this unfair world you must find an alternative way to succeed despite all challenges.

The Truth

At the point when people are stacking the cards against you, step into the storm, and make a believer out of the masses of non-believers who said it couldn't be done. You have to determine the truth for yourself and then take appropriate action. The truth is often difficult to determine, seeing that many people will alter the truth so that opportunities will swing in their favor. The truth is often hard to find, for even a broken clock is right twice a day.

I am not talking about just any truth; I am talking about the principle of "absolute truth." This simply means that on every occasion the "real" truth exists, despite what you or someone else believes. The truth is that race is just something that identifies us and makes us different from other races. The absolute truth is that when given the opportunity, some people will use race as a method to judge, stereotype, and even discriminate.

Here's another example. In my case, since I enjoy being amongst all types of individuals and learning from different cultures, I hope that discrimination is slowly going away. The absolute truth is that discrimination is not going away, and things like weight, age, gender, income, height, education, and the like are other areas where discrimination often occurs.

It is said that anytime one differs from the masses he or she is more susceptible to some form of exclusion or discrimination. Understand that discrimination does exist and will often appear when you least expect it. Be prepared to overcome this challenge when you feel you are being treated differently. Discrimination occurs daily in many different environments, such as sports, school, and work. Being that individuals often form unique bonds or cliques, they may end up treating other individuals unfairly without realizing they have done anything wrong. This is just one area of organizational behavior that is very common in groups of individuals. In these settings you may never be treated equally, but the person who wants to succeed will find an alternative path so he or she can prevail.

Diversity

Corporations and organizations often do their best to minimize these offenses by instituting diversity workshops or trainings. Diversity is a monster of a topic, and it encompasses valuing the differences of people in an effort to create a sounder, better performing workforce.

Many people in corporations feel like they do a good job of practicing diversity, but if you ask the employees what diversity means they have a hard time explaining it, and rightfully so, because diversity encompasses many different aspects, making it difficult to fully implement and execute. This is because diversity makes us step out of our comfort zones and learn something new to better the team. Many will try to simplify the issue by using another term called "inclusion." This concerns me, because the term "inclusion" makes diversity easier to grasp and is a part of diversity, but in my opinion it does not capture the complete essence of true diversity.

Inclusion says that you are including the minority or the person who is least likely to fit, but it does not mean that you value those persons, and that is where my dilemma starts with the term. If you watch nighttime television or reality shows, you will notice that all of the shows do their best to include persons of all races and genders. Do they deserve to be commended for this or not?

Many of the reality shows that we watch will have a majority white cast and then usually a combination of a black female, a black male, and one Hispanic or Asian. This is done for one reason—ratings. The networks want to make sure that they are getting support from each ethnic group and the advertisers that attempt to penetrate these ethnic groups. As a businessman I can see how this all makes terrific sense and how the networks continue to fatten their pockets, but the minorities that were added to the show for their racial background may not be appreciated and valued for their differences; they were simply added to keep ratings up.

This means that "include" is what the networks did, but practice diversity they did not. Transfer this to the corporate sector and it has even greater effect. Let's take the following situation. A large production plant has a job opening in their department. They want to fill it with a diverse candidate so they can say they are diverse, meet the diversity quotas, and look good in the nationalized ranking at the end of the year.

The company decides to hire a thirty-nine-year-old Muslim female who is highly intelligent. This person has nothing in common with her counterparts, or so they think. This young woman speaks four different languages, has two degrees, and wears traditional Muslim dressings to work, covering all of her body with the exception of her face. With all the apparent differences, no one speaks to her in the plant, so she just does her work to the best of her ability.

With no true peers, she rarely talks to anyone, and the only time she ever says a word is when the boss asks for her opinion during meetings. After she gives her opinion, seeing that she is not connected with the rest of the group, her comments are overlooked, no one acknowledges them, and the woman feels ostracized. The negative, cold feeling that she gets from these meetings makes her not want to contribute anymore and has simultaneously affected the quality of her work.

Her job is an important piece of the supply chain, and without a quality piece from her there is a bottleneck in the system, causing everyone on the line to miss deadlines. This is a case where simply "including" an individual does not help productivity or profit margins. At this point the owner of the company is upset because product quality is at its worst, revenues have fallen sharply, and if things do not improve in the next three months, the company will be forced to start laying people off. Genuine diversity training, in which everyone in the company learns to value and appreciate differences so they can all push for a common goal, would have played a tremendous role, saved jobs, and possibly kept the company profitable.

In many of my corporate trainings we have had some form of diversity initiative. Trust me when I tell you that most of these have not been very effective, but they were carried out so the company could say the employees had been briefed on diversity. Many of the diversity workshops I attended consisted only of us watching a DVD on differences and then coming back the next day with the instructor asking "Are there any questions on diversity?"

At that point we signed the form that said we had reviewed the diversity video, and we gingerly moved on. This was not true diversity training and really was counterproductive to the employees and to these well-known companies that play a very valuable part in the world's economy every day. If you are in the majority, or one of the chosen favorites in the organization, then maybe you do not see the need for diversity training, but if you are not one of the chosen few, and you are a bit different from the group, then diversity could mean the difference between you being happy as an employee or having to file a multimillion-dollar lawsuit against your company. This of course will definitely make you an outsider if you were not already.

Diversity could be the difference between your group exceeding expectations or falling drastically short of the planned goal. Diversity could mean the difference between you getting promoted for your contributions or terminated for your contributions. "The concept of diversity encompasses acceptance and respect. It means understanding that each individual is unique, and recognizing our individual differences. These can be along the dimensions of race, ethnicity, gender, sexual orientation, socioeconomic status, age, physical abilities, religious beliefs, political beliefs, or other ideologies. It is the exploration of these differences in a safe, positive, and nurturing environment. It is about understanding each other and moving beyond simple tolerance to embracing and celebrating the rich dimensions of diversity contained within each individual."[4]

Whether diversity measures are in place or not, life is not fair, and hopefully because of this chapter you do not expect it to be. During my speaking engagements I often use different stories and theories to drive a point home. I call this one the "Black Cat Theory." The Black Cat Theory simply states that many will bring you harm and ill fortune simply because of your appearance. On Halloween, many animal shelters will not let people adopt black cats. The reason for this is because of the cruelties that people do these cats as a result of their black coats and the negative stigmas that go along with being a black cat. I am sure you have heard this one: if a black cat crosses your path, then you are in for bad luck. I do not believe this, as many black cats have crossed my path, and I'd venture to guess my luck is as good as any other.

What about those who are black cat owners? Are they condemned to a life of bad luck because

4   http://gladstone.uoregon.edu/~asuomca/diversityinit/definition.html

of the color of their pets that cross their paths every day? No, I do not believe in that bad luck tale. The only one who needs to worry about having bad luck may just be the black cat. The Black Cat Theory is a cute but very dynamic way of saying that because of the way we look, our differences, and the beliefs that people have going into a situation, the minority may not get the corporate job, may not be promoted to principal of the school, may not obtain the partner status at the law firm, etc...

Keep in mind that when I say minority, I mean the unlikely fit. This could be the handicapped individual, the overweight individual, or the individual who was raised in a different country. Depending on the beliefs of the powers that be, it may be a long time coming before you get your time to shine. And even though you may want to uncover and display the truth to all those around (whistle blow), *the truth is often viewed as radical when told by the oppressed.*

So be willing to face backlash if you are exposing someone who is in a position higher than you. The key will be to find an alternative way to show your greatness. One sure way is to put on your boots, and face challenges head-on. Make it your priority to be great each and every time. Someone is taking notice of your achievements, even if you are not getting the credit for it. It may be a coworker, who five years from now will become vice president of the company. It may be a fellow teacher who ten years from now will become principal. The fact is you must always play to win, and do not be scared to take a risk, especially since life is not fair.

Life will never be fair, so prepare yourself, do the best you can, and let the chips fall as they may. Never live your life as if you have more than one of them in the bank. This is the only life you have, so live it, enjoy it, and understand that despite all its unfairness, this is still your life to win, and your success to gain. Life may not be fair, but no matter what you encounter, if you keep aiming for the top, the more likely it is that you will end up there.

Use what talent you possess:
the woods would be very silent if no birds
sang except those that sang best.
— Henry Van Dyke

TWO
....

Display Your Talents;
Then Toot Your Horn

Make your talents known. We all do certain things well, but often others need to recognize them in order for these talents to really benefit us. It is like the singer waiting for that "big break." You are not truly great until someone hears you, enjoys you, and then celebrates your greatness. You are so much more powerful once someone gives you that opportunity to shine.

The thing is, for others to see your talent, you have to take the plunge. You have to put yourself in the uncomfortable position where many will see

31

you, pass judgment, and tell others. You have to put yourself on the line and take the risk. *Boats are safest in the harbor, but that's not what boats were made for.* You must claim your success. In the corporate setting, it can be difficult to shine brighter than others. But it comes down to this: how bad do you want it?

Whose spreadsheet looks the best? Let's be honest; there are people who have earned the boss's confidence, proven they are assertive, and want to be in the spotlight all the time. Then there are those people who just show up every day, do their jobs, and expect someone to take notice of their accomplishments. Wrong. You have to *make* people notice your accomplishments, or your contribution will always be seen as marginal. As the saying goes, *the closed mouth does not get fed.*

To do this, you have to be crafty. You do not want to brag, but you want to get across the message that you are a genius in your own right. To demonstrate who you are, you must first have established a feeling within yourself that you are great, that you are brilliant. I have a saying that I use whenever I am moving into uncharted territory. It goes like this: "I am the greatest, sharpest, most dynamic person in the room until otherwise noted."

This helps me build my confidence no matter the situation. It also helps me claim my success and put myself in a position for others to admire my work. On every project I claim my success. I listen to the assignment, gather the parameters, and then start thinking to myself, how can I be the absolute best? I envision receiving the acknowledgments long before I get started.

I try to never lose sight of the desired end result, so that all my actions are consistent in achieving the goal. I think of all the ways that I can make my project the most dynamic, the most attractive, and the most powerful while staying on task. I do this so I can attempt to differentiate myself while still presenting the value proposition. The value proposition is the tangible result that I am going to create by providing my piece of the product or service. "The ability to foresee, visualize, and create your own ideas in your mind is the most powerful resource you have," said famed scientist George Washington Carver.

How do you differentiate and make your contribution relevant? You have to continuously become a wealth of information relating to your projects. If you work in marketing, then make it a point to research and share what you read in marketing publications. Perhaps once a week you send an email to the team highlighting an industry best practice that you uncover during your research.

If you are a student making a presentation on King Tut, maybe you dress up in a costume and do your presentation. If you are a teacher, perhaps you organize a school handshake that all the teachers and students learn to promote unity and school pride. If you are an athlete, perhaps you arrive an hour early for all the games and wear a tie so that you stand out. In all of these cases you have distinguished yourself from the rest of the team, who are all very talented.

Differentiate yourself without always directly tooting your own horn. Another good idea is to keep a small journal, a logbook that states what you work on daily in the course of the year. This way, when salary review time comes around, and your manager or supervisor says, "I did not see where you demonstrated the principles of teamwork," you can open your journal and politely say, "What about on March 15, when I helped organize the community service project, or on April 12, when I co-hosted the Strategic Markets Meeting?" Remember from the previous chapter that you must document everything.

It's hard to argue with that kind of detailed dated documentation. Try it—it works. How do you think I made management within three years of college graduation? I received all kinds of bonuses and was quickly placed on the fast track. Was it luck, talent, or skill? Perhaps it was a combination of all three, but I made sure that my talent was always demonstrated.

Talent

The question is what is talent? Are the guys who can dunk the ball in the eighth grade talented? Yes, and then as they move up through high school, everyone spoils them by giving them preferential treatment, gifts, and additional attention. And why is this? Is it because of their talent? Perhaps they are part of the 1 percent fortunate enough to make it into professional sports after high school. Noticing this, even more people will now run to their aid. After all, these are future millionaires, so it pays to be close to them. And these talented athletes have to trust other individuals because they probably can't manage their own affairs, especially since their whole lives people have been spoiling them. This has essentially crippled the athletes.

That was not true talent that they had; it was often a God given skill, or what many would call "a gift", and now that they are in the real world of lawyers, agents, hustlers, and sharks, they will most likely have to depend on someone else because they lack the components of true talent. They can play basketball but do not know how to prepare a resume, prepare for an interview, or type thirty-five words per minute. They cannot manipulate an Excel spreadsheet, do their own taxes, or effectively negotiate a business contract.

These are the skills that will often allow them to be successful long after their playing days are over.

As most cannot do these tasks, they are forced to depend on others. Not to take anything away from these athletes, but they are limited in what they can do, and over the long run it will hurt them. A good friend of mine, Ed West, who played fourteen seasons in the NFL, says, As athletes they often fall victim to one too many pats on the back, and after a while they start believing the hype, believing they are invincible; then out of nowhere, life has a strong way of bringing them back to reality.

How many people will they come in contact with who do not have their true interest at heart? How many millions of dollars will be squandered because the athletes feel they can just hire people to take care of their responsibilities? True talent comes in the form of the individual who did not make the team the first year but worked every minute and every hour of the summer to improve his game. Then by the time tryouts came around again, he was in shape, prepared, and had the necessary skills to make the team. This young man is no stranger to hard work, and these traits that he acquired will carry over to each and every endeavor that he attempts, whether sports or business.

There is something to be said about an individual who is not afraid to get out there and hustle, an individual who will get his or her arms and legs skinned up while learning the lesson. True talent is often not found in the person who is born with a gift, but in the person who works hard to mold his or her skills on top of his God given ability. Once a person molds skills in one area, he or she can usually duplicate the principles of hard work to improve in another area and then another and the process repeats itself over and over again. Those with true talent may never play pro sports or be the best at what they do, but they have the abilities to acquire the skill sets and to excel in just about any position they find themselves in.

Passion Versus Genius

Another way of tooting your own horn is by finding your inner genius. When asked why people are good at what they do, they will often respond "because I am passionate about my work." This sounds like a good response, and it is actually believable, because the word "passion" gives you the impression that someone is serious. But the reality is we can all do much better if we lean on our genius and not our passion. Passion has a tendency to come and go.

Many times passion comes with the surroundings. If your manager is cool, and you seem to be on top of the world, then it is easier to be passionate. If your manager is bad or does not seem to recognize your accomplishments, then that passion often dies, and you have to work like the dickens to find it again. Genius is quite different. Knowing your genius means that no matter what negative experience or setback comes your way you are capable of rising above it. You have something within you that makes you great at particular tasks and that will stay with you as long as you are breathing.

With passion, the fire can burn out, and you have to search to get it back, but with genius, you have that special trait that makes you great. With passion, you say to people that you are serious, but with genius, you show it to them. *If you want to be recognized, acknowledge your genius, utilize your genius, and while doing so, be passionate about it!*

Success will come to those who do not mind working to earn their rewards, and these rewards may have nothing to do with one's bank account. Society idolizes entertainers because of the millions that they make on a daily basis, but one must be careful to understand that all money is not good money, and money alone does not make one a success. Many people I encounter are often afraid to stand up and tell their stories because they feel they will not be appreciated, especially if they do not have millions of dollars. Do not be afraid to tell your story, as your story or contribution to society may be worth far more than any dollar amount.

As an undergraduate I was a marketing student. When I went to graduate school, the corporation forced me to study accounting and finance. For those who do not know, most marketing folks cannot stand accounting and finance. Accounting is all about numbers that are used to track costs, numbers generated from sales, and numbers used to forecast future sales. For the most part, I found accounting very boring. For me, marketing was the fun part of business, because it's all about people, products, and services.

So here I was, the dynamic marketing student who was now forced to study accounting if I was to get my education paid for. The other students who were in my class were some of the best numbers folks in the world. They came from schools like Wharton, Boston College, and Notre Dame, and from families of bankers, stockbrokers, and corporate controllers. These individuals had been exposed to financial gurus since they were babies.

Then there was me, who hated numbers and just wanted to focus on products and customers. My father was in marketing and sales, and he loved it, so why did I need to focus solely on numbers? Yes, numbers were my weakness, and they actually scared me a bit. It did not take me long to realize that I was out matched by my classmates, and if I did not get my act up to speed very quickly, I was going to be fired from my job, kicked out of grad school, and an embarrassment to myself and all the future Tuskegee University graduates that I would have blown it for, because the company would not hire any more of them based on my performance.

It was the second semester; I had failed an exam, and my manager gave me a counseling letter. One more failed exam, and I would be kicked out of school with a 3.0 GPA and immediately terminated from my job (the corporate program I was in had a 3.2 minimum GPA requirement). Now that my grades were down, my job was at risk, and my mental and physical health was decreasing, I was really feeling the pressure.

On top of this, at a time when I needed support from my classmates to stay on track, it seemed that they had turned their backs on me. No one wanted me in his or her group, no one wanted to help me with the assignments, and no one acknowledged any of my comments in class. For the first time in life, I was the ugly duckling, the weak link, and the underdog.

I remember calling my parents from 700 miles away. I would tell my dad how bad life was for me, and after he listened to me whine for about an hour, he would get off the phone, and I would start the same conversation with my mother. After two hours of complaining, I never felt any better, and my parents, though supportive, never gave me any kind-hearted words. It was as if they knew I had the talent to master my lessons as soon as I stopped feeling sorry for myself.

Being a "Player"

The only thing I had was true talent (willingness to work and learn as much as I could so that I could prevail), and my self-esteem, which said that once I got a hold of these numbers, I would become one of the best, because I already had the people skills. I enrolled in another school, Seton Hall University, to help me improve my regular coursework at Babson College where I was failing. After more exposure to finance and after taking more courses, the information began to sink in. I began to get my confidence back, and after a while I was determined to succeed. I passed all my courses at both universities and began performing better at my job and commanding the respect of my classmates. I came into my own, started presenting new challenges to my professors, and starting asking more pertinent questions. I was drawing on all my strengths to become a true business "player."

In business, a player is a person who matters, a person who makes deals come together, gets other players together, or is a key element in getting deals signed and executed. I started sending emails that reflected my knowledge of the materials, reading articles in the newspaper that pertained to my company, and meeting routinely with my managers to discuss my progress. This allowed me to show my growth, my success, and that I was not backing down for anything or anyone. I was beginning to toot my own horn.

When you get to this point, you are an extremely dangerous individual, because you refuse to let others steal your joy; you refuse to be stopped. You become a one-man wrecking crew. Your attitude is that of a superficial force that has never been seen in this world. It says, "Get out of the way, because now that I have this ball rolling, I cannot stop it, nor do I want to." On top of all of this, you just want to scream out to the world, "You cannot stop me; therefore, your best bet is to hop on and enjoy the ride." Then when you reach your full potential, you want to jump up and down and say, "Don't ever doubt me again, because when the pressure builds I'm undeniable, unbreakable, and unshakable."

You are saying "I'm LeBron James on the free throw line with no time left on the clock, and you need me to make them both." "I'm Tiger Woods on the course with a twenty-two-foot double-break putt that needs to find the hole to win the championship." "I'm Al Pacino when the studio is debating whether to fund a new hundred-million-dollar movie, and the only prerequisite is that it be a blockbuster hit." You are saying you cannot be stopped. I may have gone overboard here, but the message is that you must show the world who you are. You must toot your own horn.

As I passed the remainder of my classes with flying colors, I started to toot my own horn. I was saying to everyone, "You had counted me out, but you did not have the power to do that, because the only person who can stop Larry Jemison is Larry Jemison." Soon after I graduated from grad school I was promoted to manager, asked to lead multiple projects, and given a $10,000 increase in pay.

The underdog was now the big dog, partly because of my accomplishments, but mostly because I was able to show my managers that I was willing to put it all on the line. I was willing to achieve and demonstrate success and not afraid to toot my horn about it. When you are attempting to do great things, know that pain and suffering will come with it. If you do not feel uncomfortable about it, then perhaps you have not stretched yourself far enough. As soon as you start to feel the heat and the pain is intensifying, that is when you are truly on the path to greatness. This is when your passion and genius will be tested.

If you do not feel the heat, then you probably are not being challenged, living up to the challenge or you have not committed to the challenge. Those trials and tribulations are precursors to the success you are about to achieve, so embrace the struggles, embrace the hard times, and learn as much as you can as fast as you can. You must be prepared to work hard, fight, and then show the world that they are in the presence of a winner. You must toot your own horn but do this in a way that also shows humility. You want to demonstrate that you are capable of obtaining the results while still possessing class and dignity.

In the position I was in, there were no guarantees. I had to develop my talent and then take risks; I had to play to win. Think about life in a casino. When a person is winning, everything is great; the hotel provides him or her with complimentary gifts and free food, and everyone wants to be around him or her, but as soon as this person starts losing, the gifts go away, the groupies leave, and the gambler is labeled as having a gambling problem. There is never an issue until you are losing.

The moral is that even when you are at the bottom, your focus must be to succeed, your mission must be to win, and once you become a winner, many problems will begin to take care of themselves. At that point, you can toot your own horn once again. Just because you start in the rear does not mean you have to finish there. You must demonstrate your talents, toot your own horn, and be prepared to embrace your success!

Don't aim for success if you want it;
just do what you love and believe in,
and it will come naturally.

— David Frost

THREE
....

Believe, Create, and then Go Get It!

In the minds of many, perception is reality. You must paint the picture that you are a hard-working industry expert, whom businesspeople often label the subject matter expert. People must think that you are capable, dependable, and accountable for all your successes as well as your failures.

This is why I tend to stay away from those who believe they only have to impress themselves. They will generally make comments such as, "I refuse to jump through hoops for anyone," or "As long as I do what I'm supposed to do, I'll be okay." Wrong. *Going back to the idea of differentiating your-*

self, you should give people exactly what they expect, and then once they are satisfied, give them just a little bit more. They'll remember you for it. Many of the opportunities that will come to you will arise because someone else says you are the best person for the job.

Others' favorable perceptions of you will only help you navigate through this often cruel world. What people perceive is often what they believe. Many people believe that the World Wide Web is the gospel. Now, web sites have become more credit-worthy than many encyclopedias, magazines, or other periodicals, especially if the web sites are presented well visually. "A study by Consumer Reports WebWatch found that consumers pay far more attention to superficial and visual aspects of a web site than to its content."[5] In addition, there is a common perception that if you need to find information on anything in the world, you simply Google it. Google has created the perception in the minds of many that they are the best search engine available.

Speak Positively for a Positive Response

Another way to create perceptions is to give positive feedback to personal questions. For example,

---

5   http://www.consumerwebwatch.org/dynamic/web-credibility-reports-evaluate-abstract.cfm, Consumer Reports WebWatch, Key Findings, "A Matter of Trust: What Users Want from Websites," 2002.

when someone asks you "How are you this morning?" Your answer should always be positive and supported with energy. "I'm wonderful; if things got any better I'd have to charge admission," or, "I'm feeling super-fantastic and getting better by the minute." These are very different from "Not so good; my job has me stressed, my boss isn't fair, and my boyfriend is a jerk." In business, people rarely care if you are having a terrible day. It may be okay to speak like this with your mom or your sympathetic spouse, but other than that, check your feelings at the door. Again, you want to give the perception that if someone chooses you to perform a task, you won't let other issues impede the results. You want to give the impression that you are the absolute best person for the job.

It is also important for you to always appear busy. Remain under control but busy.

Even if you are typing the same letter over and over, others around you need to believe that you are diligently working on a task. Never be idle. In conversations, always interject that you have many things on your to-do list and that you love to stay busy. It shows dedication and accountability for your work. Others around you will perceive that you are aggressively pursuing your goals, and with that, they will respect you for your conviction. You may not get that big-time promotion, but at least your name will be in the hat.

As you establish yourself as a hard worker, others around you will begin to adopt the mindset that you are exactly that, a hard worker. They will start coming to you for help, asking your opinion on things, and wanting to be in your circle, because in the company's eyes, you're a winner. You will become a subject matter expert to many, and because of this, many above you will know your value. Even if you have a boss who is not a fan of yours, chances are if you have become the subject matter expert, someone has mentioned your name to your boss's boss or your boss's boss's boss.

So give it a little time; your climb up that ladder is soon to come. You might have to wait until your boss gets promoted or maybe even terminated, but no matter what, remember that you are responsible for your successes and your failures. So keep doing the things that make you look great.

This goes for dealing with the school system, businesses, law firms — you name it. It's important to remember that you do not own the company car, the laptop, the corporate credit card, the classroom, or anything else. This means you do not have enough invested to lose your cool and do or say something that you will later regret. Remain positive, and if anyone has to be the bigger person, make sure it is you.

Never speak poorly of another employee. Always find a way to put a positive spin on things.

Negative comments only make you look small in the long run, and they do not help you when you claim to be a team player. A prime example of this is when a great athlete is being interviewed, and the commentator says, "What do you think about so-and-so?" The appropriate response is "I think he is a great athlete, a phenomenal player, but when we square off on the court, my mission is to come out the better man." The response often given is "Well, I think he could use some work on his jump shot, and his head doesn't seem to be in the game all four quarters." Even if this is true, you have made yourself look small and unprofessional. You may not care at first, but you will wonder three months down the line why your phone is not ringing with endorsement deals.

You have painted yourself in a negative light to the world. And companies want their products sponsored by giants, people who are bigger than life, and come across as champions at all times. Give the perception that you are a winner. Winners do not bash other professionals; they find a way to put a positive spin on everything. The king of this concept is Donald Trump — well, other than his spats with Rosie O'Donnell, which could be designed to enhance his television show ratings. Donald handles the media as if he was trained to answer questions all his life. I was watching one day as the media tried to label Donald a tyrant, a money-hungry, bloodthirsty businessman who only cared about himself. Most individuals would have felt threatened and lashed back at the reporter, but not Donald. He simply smiled and told the reporter in so many words that he owns multiple businesses that employ a lot of individuals.

He said it was true that he made a lot of money, but it took money to pay all of those employees so they could support their families. He then asked the reporter how many checks *he* signed to pay others so they could enjoy a decent living. I was floored; here this man had just taken three minutes of abuse from this reporter, and then he flipped it around, kept it positive, and started talking about job creation and the empowerment of his employees to take care of their families.

The reporter was stunned and did not know how to proceed, and that was the last time he tried to attack the Donald. We can all learn a thing or two from Mr. Trump. Namely, that perception is reality. On top of this, it also pays to be a bit humble. This way you give others a reason to be proud of you instead of a reason to pull against you.

When I say you have to believe in yourself and your success, I am saying that you must envision the greatness in your mind, write it down, and then execute your plan. The easiest way to do this is to acknowledge your dreams and your goals. What's the difference, you ask? Just roll with me, because we are going to explain just that over the next few pages.

Dreams and Goals

Dreams are nothing but another form of planning, another way for you to formulate the actions you will take to become successful. Your challenge is to separate the good dreams from the bad dreams, and then commit them to paper so you can include them in your plans. How many times have you had a great dream, but then by the next day you cannot remember what you dreamed about? You may have just forgotten a twenty-million-dollar opportunity.

Who would have thought twenty years ago that someone would be able to sell bottled water for two dollars? When I was growing up, you placed a pitcher under the kitchen faucet, filled it with water, and put it in the refrigerator. Water was refreshing, and not only that, it was free! Currently, multiple companies charge for what was once a free commodity. Someone out there dreamed it and then put their dream into motion, so that people around the globe would pay for something that has historically been free. That's marketing at its best.

Back to dreams: *dreams are nothing more than vision without action.* They are things that we see but initially do not take action upon. Most of us have dreams to some capacity, but many of us do nothing with them. We use them for entertainment purposes and storytelling, but only a few of us use them to guide our lives. I do though. At this point while you are reading this book, I am living my dream. A long time ago, I had a dream that I would write a book on success and have individuals such as you—determined, passionate, aggressive individuals—read my book. So yes, you reading this book is allowing me to live my dreams.

What is the flip side of a dream? We said that dreams were visions without action, whereas *action without vision is a nightmare*. Note that when I speak of nightmares, I am speaking of conscious thought and taking action without planning, not the nightmares that people experience when they encounter rapid eye movement sleeping (or in layman's terms, "bad dreams"). Nightmares are devastating to children, families, and businesses, because they are attempts to make decisions that we have not yet internalized, prepared for, or given much thought. Many often say *success is found at the intersection where preparation and opportunity meet*. So if you have not prepared yourself and envisioned the greatness, then you are considerably limiting your chances of success.

There is another piece to the scenario. Vision without action is a dream, action without vision is a nightmare, and *dreams plus action without com-*

mitment are a fantasy. Many people will have great dreams day in and day out. We call these folks dreamers. No dreamer is too small, and no dreamer is too big. No dream is too big, and no dream is too small.

The fact is that dreaming alone will not make you successful. It can be a piece of your success, but it should be combined with actions and commitment. The dream gets you started, the action is your execution of your dream, and the commitment to make it happen is what makes a person destined for greatness, destined for success. The commitment and willingness to stick to the fight all the way through is the competitive advantage that separates the winners from the losers. Make the commitment, and stick to the fight. If you do not win, I guarantee you will learn a lot and be ready to finish at the top next time.

Dreams are very personal, autonomous, and far-reaching. Because of this, many people fear the dreams of others. This is because dreams come without boundaries, without limits, and people like to live in a world that is safe and quantifiable. Many doctors, researchers, professors, and accountants are not true proponents of dreams. These are individuals who make their money on documented proven data. These individuals depend on precise cuts, measurements, research, and numbers. They live lives that are often confined to the facts, or in business terms, the "actuals."

These individuals like scorecards, balance sheets, and proven theories, which often give them that sense of exactness that they need to feel great. There is nothing wrong with that, except for the limitations that are often placed on non-dreamers. Non-dreamers or those that deal only in the facts, often find themselves in a world full of boundaries, where the dreamers often never put constraints on what is possible. One cannot expect extraordinary results by doing normal things. It is important to find a way to reach outside the box, so you do not limit your success. When people ask you to think outside the box, you should politely ask them, "What box?" You should be thinking so broadly that you do not even see the box.

Goals are different from dreams. Goals are easily measured. Scientists, professors, accountants, coaches, and salespeople all love goals. This is because goals are measurable and easy to reward. If a salesperson reaches 88 percent of his goal, then he did not reach the goal and does not receive his quarterly bonus. If a student completes two-thirds of his assigned coursework, it's easy for the teacher to place a "C" on his report card. Very simply, goals are easy to measure and easy to quantify.

I encourage you to have goals. Though they place limitations on us, they give us concrete methods for attaining success. Goals can be short-term, medium-term, and long-term and should consistently be reevaluated and altered. A good time span for short-term goals is anywhere from one day to two years. Medium-term goals should be two to five years, and long-term goals should be greater than five years. All of these goals should be reevaluated periodically so that you are moving along at the appropriate pace and in the right direction. Your focus and ambitions may change often, so it is important to make sure that your strategies and goals are properly aligned so you are always progressing accordingly.

Make your goals real in your mind. Make a commitment to accomplish them. Do this time and time again so that accomplishing your goals becomes one of the traits that characterize you as a person. Make accomplishing your goals a habit.

No one has a right to consume happiness
without producing it.

—Helen Keller

FOUR

100 Percent of Success Is Attitude

When it comes to success, everything that you are, everything you were, and everything you are to become boils down to attitude. We have said it many times before: everybody loves a winner. Even if you are not on top of the world, you should speak and act as if you are. This goes back to perception, which we spoke about previously. People want to do business with people who are successful or appear to be successful.

The way you convey this message is to have a positive attitude and display to everyone that you are the best for morale, best for results, and best for profitability overall. You are essentially saying that you are the best thing since the invention of the drive-through. Before we go too deep into this subject, I want to highlight a major point. Many success books will talk to you about having a positive attitude. No big deal, right? But what they do not tell you is how to maintain a positive attitude when things are bad, like when you just lost your job, are experiencing a divorce, or cannot pay your bills. Attitude is most often directly correlated to the energy that you cast out into the world and a reflection of the way life is treating you. If you treat people cruelly, do not give them respect, or go back on your word, then you can expect the same in return. When this negativity comes back to you, it is usually difficult to take, so that causes your mentality to change in a negative manner. When your mentality changes for the worse, it is often very hard to regain a positive attitude, because you have created so much negative energy around you.

Let me tell you about something that recently happened to me. As an adult, I was eating the wrong foods and needed to exercise more. Knowing this, I have been lifting weights twice a week and playing basketball three times a week. I am on a health kick and getting back in shape.

This has been a great workout, and I am having loads of fun. Well, recently I was playing basketball, and my team lost, which meant I had to put my name on a sign-up sheet for the next game. After the loss everyone dashed to the sheet to write his name. One guy signed up, then I took the pen, and as I got ready to write my name, I heard someone shout, "Hey, put my name on there." A guy in the back of the line was trying to get his friend to put his name on the list before all the others had a chance to sign up. This is normal, and it happens at gyms and playgrounds all across the country, but this was different, because the pen had already been passed to me, so it was a second or two too late for the guy to get put on the list by his friend. I was about to sign my name when the guy yelled, "Give me the pen back." I quickly responded, "I'll give it to you right after I sign my name."

The young man became highly upset and snatched the clipboard out of my hand, while I was still holding the pen with the other. "Give me the pen before I slap you in here," he said. This made me smile, as I have seen this scenario play out in parks all over Chicago; Memphis; Atlanta; Pompano Beach, Florida; Plainfield, New Jersey, etcetera. If you give up the pen, then you are a punk, and the person feels like they own you.

Feeling like a punk was the least of my worries, as I knew I was man enough to handle any sort of physical altercation, but that would have defeated the purpose. I was at the gym to exercise, not to fight, and not to show who was the toughest in the gym. On top of this, neither of us had a shoe contract or were getting paid to play the game. My first objective was to let it be known that no one in the gym would be slapping me that day or any other day. The second objective was to understand why this young man had acted out with such rage.

I immediately spoke up. "Listen here, my man, you're not going to slap me, so let's get that out in the open. But even bigger than that, how did we even get to this point? What's so important about a pen and a clipboard that you would lose your temper?" The young man replied, "I'm not your friend, n---a, we ain't cool, and I don't know you, so you don't need to talk to me." I responded with, "Now you are really showing your ignorance, because no one asked who your friend was, who you were cool with, or who you knew."

The young man said, "Whatever, man, we ain't cool, and I don't have to talk to you." I agreed with him and said, "No you don't know me, and I don't know you, but that's beside the fact. I mean, we are talking about a basketball game, so why were physical threats even made? Why is it that as two African-American men, who seem to both be educated, are we even talking about physical abuse?"

The young man went on griping and moaning, and after I had shown everyone in the gym that no one was going to slap me and that this whole thing was stupid, I grabbed my bag and left the gym. My take was that it was better to leave and diffuse the situation than to push the issue further. A couple of the guys came out behind me and said, "Yo, my man, that was hot what you said back there about brothers working together and not engaging in senseless violence." To be frank, the whole stupid ordeal could have led to violence, gunplay, and innocent individuals getting hurt.

I have too much to lose to be fighting in a sports club. Not only would I lose my membership, but by the time the police arrived, I would have had to think about the possible jail time I would have had to serve, how the incident would affect my work, how my bills would get paid if I was convicted of a crime, and how the media would describe the incident. I could hear it going something like this: "Two thugs get into a brawl at a local fitness club, leaving multiple people injured."

I did not like the way that sounded, and from the way it was worded, no one would have ever known that the two individuals were prominent tax-paying citizens with college educations. I cannot confirm that the young man was a college graduate, but I assume he had at least attended college because he had a fraternity brand on his arm. So to make a long story short, two college-educated young men would have been labeled as thugs and credited with the injuries that others suffered, all over a meaningless basketball game.

I make this point only because when we see these types of events on the news, we often assume it's just more wannabe thugs causing trouble, when in actuality it is often educated individuals as well who just cannot get their lives together. It is fair to say that ignorance comes at all levels and from all places. This was black-on-black verbal assault, for no reason, but the question has to be asked, with senseless altercations such as these, will young blacks be able to work together to build strong family values? Will young blacks be able to work together to develop profitable businesses? Will young blacks be able to come together to achieve the levels of success that their predecessors did during the civil rights movement?

I am not so sure that they can, but that is not the subject of this chapter. The subject of this chapter is attitude. After this negative basketball experience, I was left a bit disappointed, and my attitude was more pessimistic than usual. I imagine that after I left the basketball court, somebody spoke up and said the whole thing was stupid; they were almost fighting over nonsense. With that level of negativity, the quality of the next few games was most likely jeopardized. That negative energy had been cast out into the gym, and because of it, what was supposed to be a friendly game of basketball was tarnished. I do not know if the young man was affected by his actions. I can only imagine that he kicked himself later for acting so unreasonably, but for me it was a defining moment in my life. I was able to voice the facts, remain composed, and walk away with no violence.

I turned a negative situation, which negatively affected my attitude, into a positive one, and because of this, the young man and I will both live to see another day. I am still proud of the way I handled the situation. Like Cornel West said, "If you want to lead the people, you must first love the people, and if you want to save the people, you must first serve the people." My job was not to fight that young man; my job was to give him some positive knowledge and encouragement, and enrich everyone else who was in the gym watching.

My job was to turn all the negative foul comments that were shouted into perishable items that possessed little to no meaning, while interjecting words of encouragement, words of value, words that would change people's lives for the better. The way I handled the situation allowed everyone involved the opportunity to come back the next day and succeed. I never did give the young man the pen back. There is a way to ask politely for the things we want in life, and since he was so disrespectful, I could not bring myself to give the pen back.

A Positive Attitude Increases Your Chance of Success

People get excited about life because of their options. Optimism comes directly from the options that we have in our lives. Young children always seem so excited, because they have so many things in life to be excited about. They have so many choices in front of them; the future alone is enough to keep them excited. That feeling of what is to come keeps them in high spirits.

Let's say the child reaches the teenage years and decides to drop out of school. He or she has just limited their options, and with these reduced options life can begin to look a lot more dismal. This negativity and lack of optimism causes the attitude to change, most of the time for the worse. Attitude has a lot to do with the choices we make on a daily basis. Other success books tell you that you need a positive attitude, but they do not tell you how to obtain it.

The lesson is simple: if you want to have a positive attitude, keep positive things in your life. If you allow negatives to creep in, then you will become negative and start to do negative things. If something goes wrong in your life, change your mindset for the better. Keep in mind that things are never as bad as they seem, and in the past you have always found a way to overcome every situation that seemed so terrible from the beginning. Remember to face challenges head-on, as this way you do not allow small problems to become larger ones.

You are human, so you will make mistakes. This is okay; just make sure that you learn from the mistake and that it is not a mistake that will destroy your life. Always think of the worst-case scenario before you take action, and if the outcome is not of your liking, then that may not be the choice that you ought to make. If your decision involves others, then be the one who always remains positive. Never do things out of spite or in an attempt to get even with someone. *The only people you need to get even with are those who have helped you.* These points should assist you in remaining positive and staying on top of your game.

On nightly television shows, when someone is having a bad day, they will often say, "I woke up on the wrong side of the bed." Never fall for that or listen to this nonsense. People do not wake up on the wrong side of the bed; they wake up on the wrong side of their minds. You see, we have a choice to make when we wake up. That choice is to be happy or to be upset. No matter what you do at that point, understand that you cannot change the things that you cannot change. Life is going to keep going whether you are mad, happy, sad, or bored. Time will not stop to wait for you to figure out how to be happy. *So for every minute of the day that you are unhappy, you lose sixty seconds of your life, the only life you will ever have.* Forget all the negatives, and focus on the things that make you happy. When an acting coach teaches people to cry, they tell them to think of the worst thing that has happened to them in life, and those thoughts begin the tear process. It is all a matter of focus. If that is the case for the negatives, then the same should hold true for the positives. If you want a great attitude, think of the positive things that have affected your life, and place your focus there.

Here's a simple method you can use to express a winning attitude. It's the art of the greeting. When you approach someone, you know what his or her first question will be: "How are you?" Now, here is an opportune time to make an impression and display a winning attitude. Many will answer with the standard "Fine, and you?" This response is so boring and so dry. Try saying this the next time that question is posed: "I'm doing super-fantastic; if I got any better I'd be triplets." It says to the person greeting you that life has never been better, and if by chance he or she has a proposition, you're prepared to receive it and execute it. It says you are the best person for the job. On top of this, perhaps the greeter was not looking for anyone to execute a project, but since you came across as being on top of the world, they may extend an offer to you. Essentially, since you have shown a winning attitude, additional opportunities may come your way. And once again we have moved toward success. *Preparation plus opportunity equals success.*

Another way of saying this is that success can be found at the intersection where preparation and opportunity meet. I have said this earlier and will continue to say it so that you understand its importance. Let's do a small exercise that shows how important attitude is in our lives. If you assign a letter of the alphabet to all the letters in the word ATTITUDE, you may be surprised what you come up with.

Here is the way this works: get a pen and paper and write ATTITUDE across the page. Assign the letters the same number as their order in the alphabet. A is the first letter of the alphabet, so assign a 1 to the A. T is the twentieth letter in the alphabet, so assign 20 to each T. You get the point. Your paper should look like this: A=1 T=20 T=20 I=9 T=20 U=21 D=4 E=5.

Add these numbers up, and let me know what you get. Do it quickly, so your friends do not get it first, but add correctly so you get the right result. Yes, that is correct; if you have added correctly, you will get 100 percent. See, I told you I was brilliant. I do not claim to be a mathematical genius, but figures don't lie; people just lie about the figures (sorry, a little golf humor).

Attitude is 100 percent of everything you were, everything you are, and everything you are to become. Attitude is defined by Webster's Dictionary as a way of acting, feeling, or thinking: one's disposition, mental set, and so on. The difference between a bad situation and a catastrophe is your attitude, the way you act when presented with a given situation.

Let's take the example of a job promotion, since we have all been there before.

You have just been alerted that the position has been awarded to another candidate. You are infuriated and go directly to your boss. You tell your boss that you are hands-down the better candidate and should have gotten the promotion. Your boss, being the politician he or she is, says "Calm down, your time is coming."

You, in a pit of rage, blurt out that your time is now, and the only reason you did not get the job is because your boss's kids and the other candidate's kids are in the same class at school. Now what started out labeled by your boss as a timing issue will now be documented as an attitude problem, chip on your shoulder, and lack of respect for authority. Do you think that you will get the next promotion with all of these negatives now on file? Me neither — glad we could agree.

Your attitude has just made a temporary, short-term decision that will have a long-lasting effect. There is no need for this. Whoever said to never let them see you sweat knew what he or she was talking about. There is never a reason to argue, raise your voice, or falsely accuse anyone while at work. Remember again that you do not own the laptop, the company car, or the company credit card.

In a situation like this, document the events, and then go through the proper protocol to resolve the issue. Your verbal skills are what got you the job, but it will most likely be your writing skills that will help you keep it. Take a deep breath, gather yourself and the facts, and let the rest fall into place. Nothing good comes out of an attitude blowup at work or anywhere else. Think smart, and keep your attitude positive. You don't want to be that parent who is carted off to jail for losing composure at the soccer game.

Understand that things are never really as bad as they seem. Think about all the bad things that have happened to you and how you felt they were the end of the world.

No matter the situation, you always made it through. You lived to tell the story. By keeping a positive attitude, you can tell the story without making a fool of yourself first. When it comes to attitude, you have to be a "player." Not the player that I spoke about in getting deals signed, but as actor Jamie Foxx says, "The player is the one who moves culture."

You see, players have a way with life, a way with people. Players enjoy each and every day, because this is their world. They understand that the world is their playground and that whether they are working or playing, outsiders cannot tell the difference, because the player approaches both with the same forward-thinking attitude.

Dr. King's Attitude

The great Dr. Martin Luther King Jr. said that a man who goes to jail needs to go into that dungeon of shame and transform it into an institution of hope and prosperity. He also said that injustice anywhere was a threat to justice everywhere. Dr. King's attitude, especially regarding nonviolence, was so moving, so forward-thinking, that nearly everyone involved began to think more positively. Dr. King was a player. His words moved so many to action, and gave others optimism when all they had before was fear of the unknown, and hope that a better day was to come.

As the years from 1968 to the present have rolled by, Dr. King's legacy is worth far more than any dollar value. Because of this man's attitude and spirit I am educated, I am a fighter, and *I will never accept "no" from anyone who does not have the authority to tell me "yes."* Dr. King has shown me that success does not come without a price. Success is often the price we pay for leadership.

Leadership may mean sticking your neck on the line and facing the harshest of cruelties even when those who were your biggest supporters turn their backs on you. Many thought King was just a rabble-rouser stirring up trouble. They did not want Dr. King to attend their churches or preach to their organizations. Many of the same folks who praise Dr. King today were those who did not believe in his dream years ago, but that is okay, as it often takes some a little longer to buy in. It is much better to be hated for who you are and what you believe rather than to be loved for something that you are not.

Great leaders usually have great attitudes. These are not the people who have simply been placed in leadership roles but those who continue to influence and lead no matter what role they have been asked to fill. The school superintendent may be a great leader, but so might the school custodian, so be aware that leaders you never even noticed may be all around you.

The Attitude of Leaders

Leaders find a way to face challenges head-on, take the abuse, and then find a way to be thankful for their success. Dr. King preached that freedom is never given, it must be taken, and this sometimes will call for the loss of human lives, but a man who has not found something in life worth dying for is not fit to live.

I was at a conference not too long ago when

Reverend Al Sharpton said, "The toughest job of a minister is to get up there and preach the eulogy of an unproductive Negro." Though he was referring to blacks at the time, this quote applies to all unproductive people. We must all look deep into our souls, and ask what we have done to make a difference. Have we spoken at a career day? Have we coached a Little League baseball team? Have we helped our children with their homework? We all have a responsibility for our own greatness but we should help others work towards their success as well.

Rap Music's Impact on Attitude

Our goal should be to become "players," those who have the ability to shape attitudes and move culture, and not only move it, but move it forward. Rap music has found a way to move culture, but often it does not move it forward. If I were a rapper with five million fans behind me, I think my next album would be about the positives that kids can have in their lives, and I would show how silly it is to buy $100,000 bracelets or glorify gun violence. I would make a mockery of this whole "make it rain" concept—of foolishly throwing cash in the air and allowing it to fall back to the earth as if it was rain, in an effort to demonstrate your success—and dare to be different. Can you imagine the company endorsements that I would receive and all the school performances I could do because my lyrics were not offensive?

You would think that this would be a great idea and that some would start doing this type of rap. Is it that they want to do it, but they know the all-powerful label will not allow it, or is it that these rappers do not have the intellectual capabilities to challenge themselves to a new standard? Will Smith is a rapper with a more family-friendly style, and he does fairly well financially. Will must have realized somewhere down the line that maybe he did not want to be shot at or that there were far more important things in life than a record sell. I am a product of the rap generation, and I love my hip-hop, but I think it is time that the rappers use their power of influence to uplift the masses and show the world they can be much more than drug dealers and heat holders (gun carriers). It is time they change attitudes and show the world that they are "players" in the business sense of the word.

What if the dress for rappers became suit and tie? Would a nation of kids respond by wanting to drop the white tees and instead pick up a sport coat? How many kids do not know how to tie a tie because their wardrobe calls for baggy jeans, white tees, and gym shoes? This again goes back to creating a perception that you are somebody. A suit and tie definitely gives off a different perception than baggy jeans and skullcaps. I am only asking you to dare to be great, at least sometimes.

If you ever want to feel good as a man, put on a nice suit, spray on some nice cologne, and walk to the bookstore, to a hotel, or to a lounge, and watch the reception that you get. People will not know whether you are the CEO or CFO, but either way, you will look and feel like a heavy hitter. I have friends who are thirty years old who do not even own a suit. Even the Grammys want you to look nice when you enter the building.

To look nice is to feel nice. It also helps to create opportunities when others see you in an unthreatening, positive light. The attitude that you are the cleanest, freshest, most polished individual in the street, the classroom, or the boardroom will make you walk with a definitive swagger, talk with an air of assuredness, and allow you to reach a level of success that may not be common to your associates. I am asking you to not just sell the product, but also become the product. You may be asking "Who is he to tell me how to dress?" Consider me your lifestyle coach, sort of like Will Smith in the movie *Hitch*!

This transition that I am preparing you for will allow you to go from the street to the suite, from Tim boots to business suits, from Elm Street to Wall Street, from playing the game to owning the team. You can become a winner, a success, but you have to be willing to change your mindset; you have to change your attitude. You will become a "player."

There are many things in life that I can do right now. I have a master's degree in business, no criminal record, and I have surrounded myself with some of the greatest friends and family that one could desire. My choices are limitless. I say all this to say, especially to you young folks, life is good; don't blow it — you can become a player. If you see someone going down the path of destruction, let them know you cannot go with them. The road to success is often found down the path less traveled.

When I was in high school, I made some mistakes, but none that would land me in jail, inflict bodily harm on anyone, or mess up my future. I had the attitude that when things got out of control, it was time for me to go. Many of my friends are still in jail for things they did years ago. I hope they get a copy of my book in prison and say "You know what? That guy always had his head on straight; he knew exactly where he was going." A wise person once stated, "If you do not know where you're headed, then any road will get you there."

To my friends in jail, I hope my attitude, that winning spirit that comes from each of these words, lifts you out of a dark sullen cell, stands you on your feet, raises your heads toward the sky, and makes you proud that we were friends. You are just good people who made a few bad choices. To the students reading this, this does not have to be you; you can achieve, you can win—just believe in these words that I am writing. You too can become a player.

I stated before that no one wakes up on the wrong side of the bed; they wake up on the wrong side of their minds. You see, at the bare minimum, you should simply be happy that you woke up at all. You passed the first hurdle by the grace of God. I read on a bumper sticker "Lord, I have not yelled, screamed, or cursed at anyone all day—now if I can just get up out of this bed!!"

Now that you are up, you must decide that today is going to be a good day, that no matter what comes your way, you will handle it with certain calmness, intelligence, and swagger. You will face all challenges head-on and make a concerted effort to have a good day. That's the way true champions do it.

Champions make a pact with themselves that they are going to do what is the best for the team, the best for productivity, and the best for profitability overall. They have something in their minds that tells them they should be at their best daily, and somewhere along the way, their body, their teammates, and fans start to believe.

But don't stop with attitude. Keep reading, because what will you do when 100 percent is not good enough? What will you do when your manager says that you have to hit 104 percent of plan to earn the additional $20,000 bonus? I know what I would do. I would focus, align my resources, drop my ego, adjust my attitude, strap on my boots, put on my hard hat, and start grinding, because there is more work to be done.

Try not to become a man of success
but rather to become a man of value.

— Albert Einstein

FIVE
....

Motivation and Politics

The Boiling Point

Let's discuss a scientific phenomenon that so many of
us take for granted on a daily basis. Let's discuss
that one-degree increase that makes water begin
to boil. At 211 degrees, water is cackling, sizzling,
stirring, and going through a scientific transforma-
tion, but that is all. Water has to go that extra mile,
gain that extra degree of temperature before it will
begin to physically boil.

Two hundred eleven, then two hundred twelve,
and like magic, the water begins to boil. It's that
one degree of separation that makes the difference.

What is your boiling point? What is that one thing that will kick you into high speed? What will get you motivated to give better than your best and more than your all?

If you have the answer to this question, then your success is not too far away. Understanding what drives you to be your best will be the difference between you barely achieving and completely blowing out a goal. American society is caught up with numbers that are multiples of ten, simply because ten is a very easy number to add, subtract, multiply, and divide. Being that 100 or 100 percent is a multiple of ten and seen as the standard for excellence, many strive to reach that bar. But what do you do when 100 percent is just not good enough?

What do you do when the company's goal is that each person will hit 100 percent, but to earn the big money, you have to reach 110 percent or better? Society has to get away from this standard of one hundred and begin to look further, begin to look deeper. The company may ask the sales force to make eight calls per day to be 100 percent complete, but for the sales rep who makes three additional calls, bringing his total to eleven per day, the odds are that he will perform better than his peers over a longer period of time.

It's all in the numbers. For many people the boiling point is money, for others family or perhaps job security, but to truly be great you have to find what will entice you to make those three extra calls per day. What is your motivation? What will make the teacher get to work sixty minutes earlier than her start time and leave sixty minutes after school ends? The fact is that you must learn to give more than expected, even if you are just giving the appearance that you are giving more. As stated earlier, this demonstrates to others that you are serious about success, which will bring you more opportunities.

The basic question is what do you do when good is not good enough? We are all good in our own minds. But what do we do when good is not good enough? When all things are equal, what makes you the best for the job? What makes you the favorite? I can bet you that the differentiator will not be that you're good. There will always be someone who is closer to the boss than you, has been on the team longer than you, and knows the job at least as well as you.

Many times you know the position better than your boss, but that is not what is in question. The difference is who can sell the idea that they are the best for the job, best for ratings, or best for profitability. Who will provide the most results for the time, the resources, and the money that is allocated? Your motto should be "When you're satisfied, that's when I'll give you more."

You should be saying "I'm going to go that one

step farther when all the others have given up." It's the willingness to push the limits so that you can be successful each and every time. Going that extra mile is what turns ordinary events into extraordinary events. Reaching the boiling point is what turns great individuals into legendary individuals. Reaching the boiling point is what separates the good from the great. Reaching the boiling point is the difference between first place and any other place.

How much would history have changed if Michael Jackson had settled for mediocrity? This guy was named the "King of Pop" because he transcended an industry (music), pioneered another (music video), and made it almost obsolete all in one. Michael turned the music world on its side when he released the hit song "Thriller." He had already achieved greatness with the Jackson 5 and his solo effort *Off the Wall*, but Michael refused to stop there.

He knew he had more to give and could do better. Quincy Jones's book describes a very timid Michael who was too nervous to sing in front of the legendary producer, but when it came down to it, Michael's drive said that this had to be done and it needed to be done right. With pressure building from his record label and deadlines to be met, Michael was forced to release what he felt was an unfinished project. When he released the multi-platinum album *Thriller*, and then the video debuted, Michael took over the world and made it virtually impossible for any other videos or albums to compare.

On top of this, he released other blockbuster hits off the same album that soon ran to the top of the charts. "Billie Jean," "Beat It," "PYT," and a few other hits made this one of the best—if not the best—pop album in history. Michael knew what it took to reach the boiling point, and just like boiling water produces enough steam to power a locomotive, Michael generated enough steam to move a world of people. People turned into Michael Jackson fanatics.

Even I refused to go to sleep at night without my shiny glove close by. Michael reached a point that boiled over and fueled almost everyone in every nation across the globe. In the 80s there was no other like Michael, and he helped many of us know what it felt like to witness success, see success, and feel success.

This type of success fuels me to do more, do better, and try harder. The majority of people want to quit as soon as the road gets a little tough, not knowing that just around the curve there is light at the end of the tunnel. *It often takes a rough sea to make a great captain.* On top of this, it is also said that the captain goes down with the ship, but the captain realizes that his ultimate fate might be death, so he will usually do everything in his power not to lose his ship or his life. It is this level of commitment: when you realize that you will not give up, you refuse to lose.

A stronger analogy may be found in a mother's love for her child. A mother will usually do anything to protect and support her child. It's a sense of commitment that cannot be put into words. If for some reason that child gets sick, needs something, or is in pain, the mother will usually do whatever it takes, including risking her own life, for the sake of her child. That willingness to fight and stand up for her child in the midst of adversity may be just enough to bring the child back to full recovery, but you can believe that the mother will not give up.

This conviction and determination is the type of motivation that breeds winners, those who only get tougher when the tides get higher and the waters get deeper. If you can just hang on, the clouds of doubt will move on, and the silver lining in the sky will show its head. If you can just hold on a little longer you will reach your boiling point. You can finish your college degrees, you can keep your family together, or you can tough it out on that job that seems insurmountable. If you know and understand the concept of the boiling point, you can make adequate changes in your life, and run long enough to cross the finish line first.

Going back to the first lesson in this book, life is not fair, so don't expect it to be. The joys and riches of sticking to it and seeing greatness in front of your eyes is worth every bit of pain and heartache that must be endured. The single mother who works three jobs and goes to school while supporting her kids knows that because she is willing to go beyond the call of duty, her kids now have a chance of survival.

The father who stays at a job where his talents are not recognized, his intelligence is undermined, and his talk of a promotion is met with laughter knows that because he sticks to the fight, the lights stay on at his house, allowing his daughter to do her homework and receive a quality education. This father knows that the boiling point is in sticking to the fight and striving to be the best, even in the face of adversity. I remember watching Michael Jordan play basketball day in and day out. The other coaches would find the best players they could to try and stop this dominating offensive juggernaut. Night in and night out, Jordan schooled guys on the court. This was not for me, not for you, and not even for his coach; Michael once said in an interview that when he played, he just wanted to be the best he could be on every occasion. And on nearly every occasion, he gave it his all. Whether hurt, sick, or double covered, Jordan found his way to the rim. He had made up his mind that he would destroy anyone who came to guard him.

His accountability for his own success gave him the competitive advantage every time. Somewhere over the course of Michael giving his best on the court, he became successful, and at this moment, many deem him the best player to ever lace up a gym shoe, including me. Michael seemed to have many boiling points in his life, and when he reached them there was nothing anyone could do to deny him. His story of success can be told time and time again in numerous ways, but when it all boils down to it (no pun intended) Michael showed us what success looks like. At some point during his career, we all sang aloud "I wanna be, I wanna be, I wanna be like Mike."

Politics in Business and Life

I will now present the concept of success in a way many other books have left out. This concept I am speaking of can be found in implementing political practices into your business plans. You probably wonder where this is coming from and why so many other books on success have left this out.

The reason this has been left out of many books is that politics scares people, it truly requires sacrifice, and it is not easy to write about. No matter the agenda or motivation, politics forces people to pick a side or stand firmly on an issue. No longer can people sit in that gray space where many love them because they are elegant with their diction or savvy when answering questions.

Politics can be the reason your business grows strong very quickly, or on the contrary, why you are still seeking your first contract. Politics can be the reason you have rampant crime in your neighborhood and schools or the reason crime is not tolerated. The political process determines who gets the best forms of education, health care, income, and housing. Politics encompasses a very powerful tool that we have all heard before but not necessarily taken action upon. This tool is called "the vote." It is a very powerful tool that many people lost their lives fighting for. Many had fire hoses turned on them by local police and fire departments, had dogs unleashed on them, and were attacked violently so that they would never earn the right to vote. If it were not a powerful tool, none of this violence would have been necessary.

What is the vote? Voting, in layman's terms, means deciding who gets how much of what, when, where, and how often. This is the simple version, which I learned from the great Dr. Martin Luther King Jr. in one of his speeches other than "I Have a Dream." If you ever get a chance, do some research on the life of this great man; he did so much more than have a dream, and because of his many words, his willingness to sacrifice, and his actions, all of us are now free to dream. I encourage you to really dig deep into his work, because the many challenges that we all face now are the same ones that he took on some forty-five years ago. Look beyond the "I Have a Dream" speech, and you may learn some key things to help you succeed in this world.

Now back to the vote. Some people in the community, usually those from low-income areas or backgrounds of less education, feel that the vote is a joke and they should not vote because it has no bearing on society. They feel that their one vote is not going to make a bit of difference in their day-to-day life. At least that is what they say, but I think that many of them are just lazy or ignorant to the facts of what the vote truly is. If I was able to speak to every single person in this country, this is how I would explain the vote.

Think about your ten favorite people. These should be people that you enjoy being around the most. They can be family, friends, teachers, or co-workers. All ten of you are in a meeting room when some rich person enters and says, "I have twenty million dollars that I am going to split between all ten of you. In order for you to get any money, you will have to answer some questions [vote], and how you answer the questions will determine how much of the twenty million you are to receive. If anyone is not up for this exercise, please feel free to exit the room right now." How many of you would leave the room?

It is fair to say that all ten people would remain in the room and try to get as much of the twenty million as possible, so why would anyone in this country not vote and try to get their fair share of the national budget? *Voting is not a spectator sport.* You cannot just sit back, watch, and then complain about what is not getting accomplished in the country.

That was just a fun example, but it is truly the same process as voting. The only difference is that there are a lot more people involved in the process of voting, and there is a lot more money (your money) involved than twenty million. We're talking trillions of dollars; if you do not vote, you have no say as to where it will go. At that point you basically have the same amount of power as slaves who were reduced to nobodies in the early 1800s. You are wasting a political tool that can aid you in funding your company, funding your child's after-school program, or repairing the streets and sewers in your neighborhood.

I hope this is making you think differently about the power of the vote and the reason we should vote. It could be the difference between the government banning a product that is the lifeline of your business or approving a product that is the lifeline of your business.

Everyone reading this book knows how important health care is to this country. You all know how much money we spend on prescription medication as well as the insurance to cover this medication. With that knowledge, you will find that all the major biotech firms and pharmaceutical companies do all in their power to influence congress to vote in their favor when it comes to reducing regulations and approving their products. Their core business, which is selling legalized drugs, depends heavily on the laws and statutes of this country. You best believe you will never hear them say that they are giving up their right to vote or that voting is worthless. Yes, you can argue that some things are not perfect when it comes to voting, but go back to the beginning of this book, when I told you that life is not fair — now get over it.

Please understand this is not a message to bash those who do not vote; it is a message that those who want to heighten their chances of success need to let their vote be heard. The older generations seem to understand this already, but the younger generation, who many say have not had to fight for much in their lives, have not bought in. Life has been good with their parents spoiling them, but when things are not so good, that's when individuals wish they were able to vote.

Perhaps when a man is wrongly accused of a crime, which happens every day, he may wish that the death penalty was not offered in his state. Had he voted, perhaps it would not have been. The vote is the only true voice you have, even though it can be a very deceptive process.

I say this because many times it is not the vote that produces actions; often it's the threat of the vote that makes people respect your desires. When politicians are speaking to the public, they always respect those who have the power to vote them in or out of office. So if a particular group has numbers of potential voters, then the politicians have to address the issues and desires concerning that group. Remember, the vote determines who gets how much of what, when, where, and how often. It is a powerful process, and those who do not cast their ballots on voting day are saying they are content with their lives and not looking to improve their conditions, ignorant to the facts and do not feel like their life is worth improving, or have been convicted of a felony and their voting rights have been revoked.

The citizens of the U.S. who make a lot of money and are highly successful believe in the vote simply because it is in their best interest. They know that if they are a threat to vote a politician out of office, the issues that affect their communities will be heard. These can be issues such as tax increases and decreases, gay marriage, abortion laws, after-school programs, road repairs, and crime rates. We could turn this into a whole chapter, but we will not.

This was just another issue that I wanted to share with you, so you can enhance your chances of being successful. The vote is your voice, and the threat of the vote is what calls politicians to action. These are the actions that can turn a small business into a large corporation, that can turn vacant land into housing developments, that can turn a sixteen-year-old "C" student into a twenty-eight-year-old surgeon, engineer, or lawyer. It all depends on what issues were voted on to give each individual their fair chance at success, with the word fair being relative.

Find something that you are passionate about, and stand up for it. That is what sacrifice is all about. Be passionate about it, and take refuge in the fact that you have something you feel strongly about. Once you are passionate about it, you can make it your own, cherish it, and protect it. It will become your cause.

> *Passion comes from the heart and is manifest as optimism, excitement, emotional connection, determination. It fires unrelenting drive. Enthusiasm is deeply rooted in the power of choice rather than circumstance.*
> —Stephen R. Covey

The difference between a boss and a leader:
a boss says, "Go!" — a leader says, "Let's go!"
— E. M. Kelly

SIX
....

True Leadership in Society

This chapter is dedicated to those individuals who are not afraid to step up and make the wrong decision, knowing that no matter how things turn out, they will stand by their decision and be accountable for the results. Very few people are willing to stand up for their decisions, which makes them cowards and definitely not leaders. In discussions and meetings around the globe, individuals want to be considered "the man" or "the woman," but very few people want to be held accountable for what happens based on their decisions.

It is all fun and games until your decision makes your company lose twelve million dollars, is the reason 10,000 employees lose their jobs, causes 26 percent of your students to drop out of school or 5,000 troops to lose their lives. These numbers are tough to hide from, and the end result is often failure. You become seen as either a hero or the biggest loser in history. In many situations it is possible to be seen as both simultaneously, depending on who benefits or suffers. You see this with American presidents. Many will praise the president, because their company benefits from a decision that the president has made, while others complain about the president's actions, because the decision may take funds from their company or household. This is what leadership is often about, making the tough decisions that affect many and having to live with those decisions, be they good or bad. If you want to become successful, you will need to break away from the norm and step out into the fire.

The masses are not going to tell you this. They would much rather you be a note-taker and follow the initiatives of others. You become normal when you do this, and others around you love normalcy. Leaders know how to mix things up a bit and go wholeheartedly for their dreams. You cannot expect extraordinary results by doing normal things.

Many individuals go their whole lives wanting to occupy the number one position. They desire to be the boss, but for all the wrong reasons. They want to be the boss because they see life is tough, and they think it will be that much easier if they are the ones calling the shots and telling others to do all the heavy lifting. I hear it all the time, individuals commenting "I can't wait until I'm the manager; I'm going to really show them how to be in charge." Get ready, because these types of individuals are terrible for business, ruin employee morale, and will account for the rapid turnover that your organization is about to experience. They're power hungry versus results focused.

Leadership is not what you do to me; it's what you do with me. Though someone may be higher than you on the ladder, you want them to know that when you go to battle, you are right there with them. That's what makes an organization strong. A football game is not about getting eleven men to score the touchdown; the coach has to find people who will block, tackle, run, pass, kick, and anything else needed to move the chains down the field. Once all this happens, and the team is in scoring position, they usually go to one of their strongest offensive forces to get the ball across the goal line for the score.

The coach is less concerned with each player becoming the hero and more concerned that they all work as a team to achieve the common goal of scoring the football. Then once all the blocking, tackling, and running is completed, and the time runs off the clock, the team can celebrate, as they all have become winners. Many in corporate America and in education would achieve unforeseen levels of greatness if only they could internalize this concept of working together as a team.

This is a tough concept to teach because of all the different social classes in America. People grow up working for others, feeling overworked and underpaid. It is the difference between the haves and the have-nots. After being the servant for so long, a feeling of struggle and being tired of working for others sets in. People in this situation eventually want to be the leader, and as they strive to the top, they rarely forget how they were treated, but instead of breaking the mold and changing once they succeed, they often become exactly what their superiors were.

We were just talking about how powerful the vote is. Let's go one step further with that. I know individuals who will vote the same way their neighbors voted just so they won't be the misfit at the community pool. If you ask them why they chose a particular candidate, they have no earthly clue why they voted that way. They don't know what issues the candidate supports, they haven't read any information on the candidate, and they haven't watched any debates, but they figure if they vote like the masses, then they are safe. Again, this country is lacking in the leadership department. I don't care if you vote Democrat, Republican, or independent, but I do care that you vote and know why you vote for a particular candidate.

A new era in leadership is emerging, because children are becoming more entrepreneurial in their management styles. Many are not interested in working for anyone, and they do not want to work for years to achieve the things that they want. These children want the finer things in life, and they want them now. This sense of urgency has caused the more traditional style of leadership to fall by the wayside.

Much of this assertiveness has come from the hip-hop culture. Though negative values are often associated with this culture, hip-hop has created a breed of new young entrepreneurs like we have never seen before. In addition to this, with the enhancement of technology, young people are able to start businesses and run them right from their laptops without having to leave the house. This means that companies will soon need to assess their management styles to see if they can function using the age-old hierarchical system that has become commonplace.

This new-age leader is refusing to work for the same company for thirty years and retire through the 401(k) program. These new-age employees are becoming more educated, and they realize that they have more options in this dynamic economy. They also realize that the job they currently have may not be around in ten years, so they better have a backup plan. It is a shame that these brilliant minds are coming out of college and being assigned the roles of paper pushers for the higher-ups. These brilliant minds do not feel they are being allowed to develop at the rate they would like to.

This in turn creates a nation of disgruntled employees who know they can do more and produce better results. These individuals are often very talented, and instead of being hired on as an asset, they are now viewed as threats by management and will have to jump through more hoops than what they feel is worthwhile. After seeing limited growth potential, the employee will decide to leave the company, costing the company money and leaving the company with a position that they will have to re-hire and re-train someone for. The company will suffer in the long run, but on a local level nobody seems to care, because local management was simply trying to save his or her job versus maximizing overall potential.

The Challenge of Being a True Leader

The school system is the same way. I have spoken with many teachers, and most of them say they are not allowed to be true leaders. When a teacher comes in with talent and skills, the administrative staff often views them as a threat, and even though they are good teachers, they end up feeling intimidated by the assistant principal. And the principal often views the talented assistant principal as a threat, and the assistant principal ends up intimidated by the principal.

The principal is talented but governed by and afraid of the superintendent. The superintendent is hesitant to put his or her foot down in cases where a student may need to be disciplined because they are afraid of the parents, and the parents are afraid to be parents because they have kids who are not afraid of anybody. The end result is that we have a school system that is often failing our kids, and we are all to blame. We can no longer explain the causes of why something does not work in the school system; we must find ways that will work. Success is the only option, or someone's kid will fall behind and often never recover.

The fact is that leadership is falling by the wayside. There seem to be very few true leaders left, and the leaders that are said to lead today seem to be there because of their finances. It appears that whoever has the largest pocketbook gets to lead. It seems to never fail: as long as you have money, this country will justify why you should be in a leadership position.

I don't buy into this concept because I still have the ability to think for myself. I know that many will try to mislead others for their own personal gain or benefit. To become a leader you will need to think for yourself as well, not saying that you may not agree with the masses, but never take drastic action without giving it some personal thought. Life comes down to the decisions that we make.. Outside of politics, can you name five leaders? This is something to think about, as we claim to be a country that encourages leadership, but where is it? It is time for us to execute and ensure that opportunities to lead are given to qualified individuals, not just the people who make a lot of money but have no true governing skills.

We have artists who drink, drive drunk, and cause accidents. Then they are nominated for all kinds of image awards. We have many members of the church, all the way up to the ministers, who are abusing their power and using God's name to manipulate others. This is documented, and many followers still won't stop to think for themselves.

Many people need to find their spirituality and combine that with their religion. Dr. Calvin Mackie said "Religion is for people who are afraid to go to hell, and spirituality is for those who have already been there." Many people hate for you to criticize the so-called leaders, but I am not afraid to call so-called leaders to the carpet when they are wrong. This goes back to earlier parts of this book where I state that we need to be accountable for both our successes and our failures. I may respect a person for being on television and being in the public eye, but if you are wrong then you are wrong, and I am not afraid to bring it to the light. This does not mean that my comments are personal; it's just that if we are to become better, we must highlight areas in which we are not achieving the desired goals.

One of the only places we may see true leadership is in the business of athletics. Notice I said "the business of athletics," not "the athlete." These highly paid athletes are accountable for success and putting fans in the seats. You can be a great athlete, but if the stands are not full, then the owner's job is to get other personnel out there to fill the seats. Once the appropriate personnel are enlisted, then those are the people who will be on the field, and those are the people who will be rewarded.

Another place where you may witness true leadership is in small businesses. Small businesses generally do not have an abundance of money or additional resources to hide behind like that of the large corporate manager. The small company owner must get the most out of every resource and every dollar just to stay in business. The small business has to fight to stay alive in a competitive environment, or it will fold.

The bottom line is that there are very few true leaders. The same guy who claims to be a true leader is also the person who will turn and run at the first sign of trouble. He is the same person who will quit as soon as the road begins to get a little rocky. Most people will give up before the fight has even begun. I advise you to stick to the fight, because just being in the race means that you have a fighting chance, and when the other guy gives up, you have moved that much closer to success.

Everyone wants to be the leader, the top of the class, but leadership comes with responsibility. It is not always glamorous, it is not always fun, and it often comes with a price. What price are you willing to pay to lead? Jesse Jackson says that no one has the right to give less than their best. He said this is because others before you have paid the price.

Martin Luther King Jr. paid the ultimate price; he died so others could have a chance to lead. I take this seriously and am committed to preparing my mind on a daily basis, so I am prepared to lead. If you too want to be successful and want your fair shot at leadership, you must keep thinking for yourself, gaining as much knowledge as possible, and separating yourself from the nation of followers who would rather have someone tell them what to do versus create their own path.

Accountability in Hip-Hop

Recently, radio and television host Don Imus was terminated for referring to the Rutgers women's basketball team as "nappy-headed hoes." Many individuals were split in their opinions on whether the firing was appropriate. Then the controversy went from Imus's comments to the world of hip-hop and the number of artists who use the same types of degrading slogans throughout their music. I'm going to tell you how I feel about the situation, only because it needs to be stated. It pertains to my being a leader, and it all ties back to accountability.

Many ask why the Don Imus controversy shifted from Imus to the hip-hop generation, as if the two incidents are totally separate and detached from each other. In my opinion the incidents are separate, but the issues are not detached. We all must be accountable for our actions, and that goes for corporate Americans, disc jockeys, parents, teachers, entertainers, and the list goes on and on. I will focus on the hip-hop artists though, since the Imus issue was compared to hip-hop music.

Now, for you to see where I am coming from, you must separate yourself from being a hip-hop fan, from being a hip-hop artist, and from anyone who profits from the sale of hip-hop music. Just for a couple minutes, I need you to clear your mind, and try to see where I am coming from. Over the years I have grown into a true fan of hip-hop. I have done so because the music is a product of my generation, and it has provided the artists freedom of expression, while making a few of them wealthy beyond their belief.

Notice that I said beyond their belief, because even though they have made good money, they have still been tragically ripped off. The theft starts from the manipulation of their time and their talent, and then of course there is the money. Anytime someone offers you pennies on the dollar for work that you create, please understand up front that you are probably getting ripped off. This is okay, as business often involves manipulation, but you should at least know what you are getting into.

Before we go too far with this, understand that music is just another form of business in which products and services are sold. It has its own twists and turns, but music is about creating, marketing, and selling products. You can create, sell, and market any product and be very successful, even more successful than in music, because hopefully your business contracts will benefit you a lot more than that of the standard record deal. If you sell a million Frisbees, you can make a significant profit; it's just that the music game is so well publicized and glamorized that it looks so much more attractive. Trust me when I tell you it isn't. All that glitters is not gold — or should I say platinum?

The hip-hop culture involves more than just music. One mainstream rapper said "Rap is what we do, but hip-hop is what we live." Hip-hop is the lingo, the clothes, the politics, and the complete movement of a generation. It is a movement that has inspired and motivated young folks like never seen before. I applaud hip-hop for instilling this desire to succeed in this younger generation, but just as in business, we must hold these individuals accountable for their success and failure.

In so many areas that hip-hop has succeeded it has also failed. Most of the artists have gone to a far degree of rapping about violence, degradation of women, and promotion of illegal substances. On top of this, the lyrics are raunchy, to say the least, and they glorify the "N" word as if the thousands of slaves who suffered because of it never existed. Most artists could care less about slavery, and if asked to simply name five slaves who were not featured in the movie *Roots*, most would have trouble doing it.

The end result is a nation of children who can cite every word of a rap tune but often can't spell "diploma." If they put as much energy into their lessons as they do into listening to rap music that is non-progressive, they could be educated and still have the option to rap, versus putting all their eggs in one basket, and when that does not work out, they are left with few options to succeed. Rap music is not bad. Hip-hop is not bad. It's just that many of the lyrics that are contained in these songs are negative, raunchy, and do nothing to uplift the masses. This is not to say you are not motivated after listening to one of these songs, but what are you motivated to do?

Many say that since hip-hop is entertainment, it is okay to degrade and use horrible language, as long as you are just entertaining. That is a lie. Remember the earlier quote saying rap is what we do and hip-hop is what we live. Well, if you are living this, then it has now gone from entertainment to reality, and for many children this will be the end of their lives. Tupac Shakur once said, "I wonder if heaven got a ghetto?" The sad part about that is he got his answer before he was even close to thirty years of age.

The glamour, glitz, and perils of hip-hop literally claimed his life, while for others the destruction will come more slowly, over a period of years, when success eludes them because they did not prepare themselves during the learning stages. My take is that we are all accountable for what comes out of our mouths, no matter the occupation or the purpose. If we say something that is offensive, then we should be accountable for it. If we say something that is derogatory, then we should be accountable for it, and the law of attraction says we will, because what we put out into the world and what we focus on will come back to us.

There are no free passes because you are a rapper, comedian, or television host. I understand why those in the rap world would not agree with my logic, because they have to protect what pays their bills. And if they do not rap, what else is available to them? Will they be able to open their own law firms, attend medical school, or become CPAs? I doubt it, as they often describe music as their only ticket out of the hood, or so they think, so they keep providing what the market demands.

Rappers, your words are more powerful than you can imagine. You truly are shaping the minds of tomorrow, but are you filling it with garbage that will ultimately ruin a lot of children? Remember, many of these children do not have adequate parents at home, so they are using your lyrics as the blueprint to success. I remember growing up in the 80s. There were plenty of rappers, but they were so creative that they did not have to be raunchy and degrading like they are today. I do not want you to think that I am coming down on the rappers, as like I said before, I am a fan when the music is creative and inspiring.

Here is where the twist comes in. Every great book has a twist. I mentioned a few paragraphs earlier that rappers have to keep bringing what the market is demanding. This means that people are still buying this trashy rap, so the artists will keep making it. It's simple supply and demand. When this negative rap gets to the point where people do not appreciate it anymore, consumers will stop purchasing it, and the rappers will then stop making it, but as long as consumers are purchasing it, rappers will continue to make it.

With that being said, the responsibility ultimately falls on you, the consumer, to demand a better product, products that will uplift and make you feel good about society, products that you would not mind your kids listening to. Most individuals would not be willing to say what I have just said over the past few paragraphs because it goes against the norm, but I have no problems with it, because I am one of the few "true leaders" who will stand up for progression and the younger generations. The music business is an ugly game, and I do not have time to tell you how it really goes down, but I advise you pick up a book called _Hit Men_ by Fredric Dannen before you jump into it.

So should Imus be held responsible for his words? Without a doubt, but so should the hip-hop generation that believes because it's just entertainment it's okay to be raunchy. We have a priority to protect our kids. Adult films are viewed as entertainment as well, but those XXX labels are there for a reason. Just as R-rated pictures are off-limits to minors, so should be these raunchy CDs that are affecting the children. Just because it's entertainment does not mean it does not have to have social accountability. If not all the lyrics are cleaned up in rap, there should be at least some kind of balance, in which half of an album is fueled with substance.

The consumer has an obligation to buy material that is worthy of purchase. The large retailers should have some social responsibility as to what they will sell in their stores, and the record labels need to clean up their rosters so that quality products are coming out of their studios. If not, once the consumer decides that enough is enough, or as stated in other words, that "hip-hop is dead," record companies, retailers, and artists may find themselves suffering from huge deficits.

No need for panic just yet, as this new nation of leaders will probably not hold you accountable for the next few years, but once this book drops, I can make no promises. Just as you are influencing minds with glamorized quick-money schemes, illegal drugs, and degradation of women, I am here to promote education to the masses, social change among aspiring entrepreneurs, a worldwide campaign against drug use, encouragement of individuals to become leaders, and the uplifting of the most beautiful creation of all, the woman.

The Most Powerful Word in the World: Money

We have just spent a good bit of time talking about social accountability and being responsible for our words and actions. Nothing in the last few chapters was too difficult to comprehend, but there is one concept that seems to either add complexity to all situations or smooth out all situations; it just depends on which end of the couch you are sitting on. This is the concept of money. Let's take a moment to get a little closer to the concept of money and its power to shape or destroy leaders.

This book is all about success, and how can one talk about success without talking about the number one standard for measuring success, right? Money is such a powerful thing: it makes the rich feel they have more power, it makes the poor feel they have to do foolish things to get it, and it makes the middle class feel that if they could only make $500 more a month, they would be on top of the world. Money is such a simple means to measure artificial success. I call it artificial success because most of the time those with money are no happier than those without it.

As P. Diddy once proclaimed, "More money, more problems." Some characterize money as the root of all evil, while others say it's the lack of money that is the root of all evil. No matter what your belief, we will take a closer look at this concept that we have all grown to know and love.

Money is nothing more than a medium of exchange, a way to pay for products and services that are rendered to you. It is simply termed currency, but this currency comes with immense power, because every person around the world has come to respect its capabilities. It has become a universal language spoken around the world, and no money has as much brand recognition as the U.S. dollar.

I do not care what country you travel to: you may not be able to speak the native language, but as soon as you pull out the dollar bill, the merchant will usually know exactly what you are saying. They understand the economic principle of exchange rates; they know how much of their currency equates to that one-dollar bill.

In the USA, 8,000 sheets of money are printed every hour. The actual currency is comprised of 75 percent cotton and 25 percent other contents. Out of the 8,000 sheets printed every hour, the ink is put on the paper by the ton, not the gallon. Out of these, there are some defects, and the Fed destroys twenty-eight million bills per day. On top of this, more than 100 million fake dollars are being used worldwide, with 39 percent of this fake money being done on home computers, scanners, and the like. People have become obsessed with money, and it is said that there are more than 6,000 bank robberies per year.

The people give money its power. If no one placed a true value on the dollar amount, then the U.S. dollar would be virtually powerless, but since we know how many dollars it takes to buy dinner, a new car, or a new home, the currency continues to have value, and socially it really does separate the men from the boys. Not only this, but many people have come to equate money with success, which is a common mistake that I want you to move away from if you share that belief.

Use money as a means to obtain the things you need to survive in life. Use money as a means to acquire services you need to improve your life. Use money as a scorecard of where you are in reference to financial security, but do not use money as the sole record of how successful you are. I know a lot of people who have loads of money, but they would trade it all in to have a better relationship with family members, have true friendships, or cure the cancer that has taken over their body.

Unfortunately money cannot buy the love you desire, and money cannot buy you a clean bill of health. Money is just the means to purchase goods and services when you deem them either wants or necessities. Most people have been using money for so long that they envision just a few more dollars will make them happier, but the fact remains that it will not.

Most people blow money every month whether they have it or not. This happens whether you are a doctor making more than $200,000 a year or a teacher making less than $40,000 a year. The fact is that most people waste money even though they worship it. If the money was what would truly make them happy, then they would do a better job of saving and investing versus spending reck-lessly. We all have wasted money, and the more we make, the more we often spend, when it should be the more we make, the more we save. Note that this is the common person's guide to success, as Donald Trump would not buy into this save sce-nario, because he makes money by initially taking on more debt and turning that into a nice return, but for the common persons, we need to focus on saving more.

This society is one that craves power, and many feel that money gives them that extra power, power meaning the ability to determine outcome. This is true in many cases, but the power that you crave can be the same power that destroys you and in turn makes you unsuccessful. It is important to understand that money is the reason companies are started. Money is the reason that people go into business for themselves. They have a desire to make a lot of money.

This is an accepted theory, and if you go into business, know that you are going into it to make money. If you are not going into it to make money, then you are not going into business; you are going into a hobby. Make sure you know the difference. Business is about making money, but again, this money is not always an accurate depiction of suc-cess, and there are many other things to consider.

Plenty of companies make money, which is a

good thing, but as we go down through the income statement and see how the expenses add up, by the time we get down to the bottom line, there is no money left for profit. So again, we go into business to make money, but if there is no profit to show at the end of the day, then the business is not successful. Many people will use money as an indicator, because others who are outside looking in will automatically relate money to success.

Have you ever been to an awards banquet or dinner party where they introduced the speaker as a person whose business does $2,500,000 in revenues every year? You automatically start to wonder what type of car the person drives, how big their house is, and how much money they make per year. The reality is that the company may generate $2,500,000 in revenues and have expenses of $2,200,000, and the additional $300,000 must be used to pay employees and keep the business going. With that said, the person may not have a nice car, big house, or nice salary. The money, again, is not an indicator of success.

In earlier chapters we said that people often justify people who have money, or who seem to have money. If we know that someone has made a lot of money, inherited a lot of money, or is close to someone with a lot of money, then we will often justify them as a person of distinction. We will begin to justify that person simply because they have money. We will find a way to make this person a leader. That is not the way I do it, as I call it like it is. I believe most people are good people with the option to do bad things, so when they start to think about ways to make money, that is when their morals and values tend to go out the window.

Many people make a lot of money, but not all money is good money. Drug dealers make a lot of money, but look at the dangers they put their family members in, look at what they are doing to their communities, look at the kids that follow in their footsteps. The money was the root cause of why the drug dealer began "hustling" in the first place. I do not care how much money the drug dealer has; I refuse to justify his or her actions because they have financial wealth.

The Challenge of Leadership in the Hip-Hop World

Slavery makes money, but I do not believe in enslaving any person for any reason other than punishment for crimes they commit. Historic slavery was the foundation for most of the millionaires who were based in the Old South. They used their slaves to work the land, pick the cotton, and grow the tobacco. Many of these businesses are still in operation today and still enjoy huge profits stemming from the dollars they made during the time of slavery. This is yet another example that not all money is good money.

Many rappers in the world of hip-hop make a lot of money. But as of 2007, many of them are still signing recording contracts that pay them less than twenty cents per album sold. This is not only the new rappers; these are also seasoned rappers who have a strong following. They are basically getting ripped off due to their own ignorance pertaining to contracts.

This is not a personal attack on rappers or the other artists, but like I said before, I call a spade a spade. And since this book is entitled *How to Make It in a World That Wasn't Made for You*, it is my duty to educate. These rappers have a strong base of people that will buy their records, DVDs, and promo items based on their names alone. That being said, many of them do not need a recording contract at all, especially one that does not pay.

These artists would do much better by doing independent music promotion, selling fewer copies, but earning much more per copy sold. Plus, with the flexibility of not being tied to the record labels, they would have much more freedom to do soundtracks with others, make money on their own promotional items, and secure more lucrative acting gigs. The rappers do not have to get angry at my comments, but they can use them as a wake-up call; tell them to call me, and we can work on making them true millionaires.

Any artist who wants to go further with this

and talk about how they can make more from less is welcome to contact me. No need to let your pride get in the way of you making more money — I mean after all, you are already willing to say just about anything on a recording, as well as make videos that demean others, so let the pride go and reach out to me for some ideas. *At the end of the day, even Tiger Woods has a coach.* This is not the purpose of this book, so I will get back on track, but I had to add that to show how much these artists are getting cheated year after year.

Now that we are back on track, let's talk about rap again and the money that is made from rapping, which at this point is nothing more than further exploitation of the younger generation, which corrupts the minds of those who otherwise may have tried to do something with their lives. Rap music as it stands right now is an alternative for those who do not educate themselves at an early age but still want to achieve financial gain. It goes back to that principle of trying to receive something for nothing.

Do not confuse my words. I am not saying that I have anything against rap music, but I am saying that there is a definite lack of substance being recorded, and there is nowhere near a balance in the content. For every one rapper that encourages students to go out and become somebody, there are 2,000 who promote drug dealing, gun violence, and an endearment for the term "n---a," which is a term of hatred that many died for. I feel that we are shaming the efforts of those individuals who lived and died so we could have an opportunity to prosper. When will we wake up? Or will we not, because we are again blinded by money?

Many of the rappers you think are successful are still living with their mothers, renting cars for their videos, and renting the jewelry that they brag about. The music business is one of the most corrupt businesses out there, and if parents knew like I do, they would encourage education and discourage celebrity. Jay-Z says on his album *Kingdom Come* that fame is the worst drug known to man.

It is time that we stand up and realize that just because it makes money does not mean it's right. Answer this question: how much would you pimp your kid out for? That question alone should make you understand that money is not everything. Then again, how many people would get this answer wrong too?

It is time the true leaders stand up and take their positions. It is time we demonstrate proper leadership to our kids versus just telling them about it. Leadership is a concept that is falling by the wayside in our country, and as stated above, it cannot all boil down to money. Some of the best leaders of our times did it because they loved the people and because money was not the motivation. They could not be bought, which allowed true uncorrupted leadership to take place as well as unbiased scientific discoveries to be unveiled. Do we live in a world that values great leaders or good followers? That's food for thought.

The most important single ingredient in the
formula of success is knowing how to
get along with people.
— Theodore Roosevelt

SEVEN
....

The Power of Relationships

Many times who we become or the opportunities that come to us are directly correlated with who we associate with. I have noticed in my business life that those who attend Ivy League schools often fare much better than those who attend regular four-year institutions. My assessment of the reason for this is that the Ivy Leaguers stick together within their network and help each other overcome what would ordinarily be barriers to doing business.

The network that I speak of is only as strong as the individuals in it; therefore it can be beneficial or detrimental to your success. We often read that people come into our lives for a reason and a season, meaning they have some purpose in our lives, but once that purpose has been fulfilled, they will often fade out of our lives. This may be the best thing to ever happen to you, because some networks are not sound and not built on strong foundations such as integrity, accountability, and willingness to compromise.

We often speak about great networks such as the sports team that constantly wins the championship, the sales team that always breaks the revenue records, or the businessmen and women who make up the local chamber of commerce. These are all seen as positive networks in which success seems soon to follow. It is extremely important that you choose your networks wisely.

I spent part of my high school years in Pompano Beach, Florida, and the rest just outside Chicago. In both areas I had the opportunity to hang out with some questionable characters. Seeing that I was personable and a good athlete, I was quickly accepted by the scholars who did well in school and the jocks who were seen as popular as well as the thugs who ran the streets.

In many cases the networks start to cross over into other areas. Due to the fact that all accepted me, I was comfortable in all settings, but I knew my limits. When I was playing basketball at Gunderson Park, I enjoyed everybody, scholars, athletes, and thugs alike, but as soon as signs of trouble presented themselves, I quickly retreated from the court and usually went straight home. At sixteen years of age, separating from what seems like the cool crowd, or your friends, is a tough thing to do, but many of those guys who were my friends were often arrested, beaten up, or shot, just because they stuck around when trouble came.

My future was too bright to be ruined by one mistake, so as soon as I saw trouble brewing, I left. As I look back over the past fifteen years, many of those guys are still locked up, and they tell me the same old things: "Had I been more like you, my life would have been much better," or "As soon as I get out of here, I am going to get with you so I can get things straightened out." It's just too bad they had to spend ten to fifteen years behind bars before that thought was clear.

As soon as you see signs that you are beginning to go down the wrong path, please take the time to evaluate yourself and your surroundings. One path leads to greatness, to success, while the other may just lead to jail, poverty, or death. For you kids, listen, and listen well.

Keep your network strong. When you see trouble coming, distance yourself as quickly as possible. You are not considered a wimp in any way for leaving the area, but you are a wimp if you do not use your mind to analyze the situation and get away in order to ensure you reach the greatness you are on track to attain.

Choose Your Network Wisely

The more you experience life the more you will notice that people are in your network for many different reasons. This could be because they work closely with you, because your kids play together, or because they are fun to be around. Make sure that the people are good people, so that they do not get close to you and then betray your trust, which often happens in close-knit circles. This is often easier said than done, but as you live, you will become better at evaluating who is sincere and who is not.

Do not let a person's status in the community, the type of car they drive, or the amount of money they make determine whether they should be in your circle. I know a lot of people who had nice homes and cars years ago, but now they are broke, friendless, and begging others for assistance. Many times they were not good people themselves, were not good friends, and were not approachable, even by the people who cared the most about them. So as they continued to make bad decisions concerning their network, their whole lives spiraled down before them.

There are two sides to every circle: inside and outside. Be careful who you let in your circle, as negative people in your circle can be as debilitating as any rare disease. You must protect and constantly evaluate your circle, so your success is never compromised by poor relationships.

Many times the reason a person cannot get a business off the ground is because they do not have the resources or the startup capital, but if you have the backing of someone who is in your network, you will now have access to resources that the common man may not have, further raising the chances of your company's survival. There is a special force that comes into existence when all parties involved are focused and working toward the same goal. It has been said that one spider can spin a web strong enough to support the spider, but 300 spiders coming together can spin a web strong enough to tie down a lion. There is an even more incredible force when people come together for a common goal, and each person knows they can depend on the other to do their part.

My friend Hotep, author of *The Hustler's 10 Commandments*, says that your NetWORK equals your NetWORTH. The more and more I close big business deals, the more I realize just how true this statement is.

Relationships are key when it comes to success, because most of the things we want to do in life require someone else. There are very few things that we can do entirely by ourselves. I notice that people who are successful in real estate usually have good rapport with the mortgage companies, the closing attorneys, and the banks. I notice those who are successful in sales usually have good rapport with their customers, the service department, operations teams, and their sales managers. Those who succeed in education usually have good relationships with the teachers, administration, and parents.

The relationship is the edge that allows success to enter the equation from many different areas. Donald Trump says that some of the best investments he ever made were the ones that he passed on. He also says that he has a team of individuals that he counts on to make the important deals and that he rarely deviates from those individuals. Donald has found a certain level of trust within those folks, as they have proven that they can produce the results time and time again. Since Donald has the relationship with these specific individuals, he is often noted for finishing projects before the deadline as well as coming in under budget.

Many times those who start new businesses will apply for loans or try to secure outside financing. Seeing that the business is new, there is no real track record to judge the potential for success or the creditworthiness of the individual. This often means that the loan request will be denied. The lender wants to know that you are credible and will be able to repay the debt.

This is when it may be a good idea to add a new team member who has a more proven track record. The banks, outside investors, and credit agencies will often look at the history of the new member and then extend credit to the company. This is the way it is, and if you want to get in the game, it helps to have dynamic, positive individuals on your side. It helps to have an efficient network.

You must also learn from your relationships and recognize when they are beginning to sour. You may have known a person for many years, but you never truly know a person until they betray you. If they never do, excellent; you can continue to run business as usual, but when they betray you, you must decide the next course of action, and hope that half of your company does not belong to them. When times are good, they can be really good, but when they go bad, they can be really bad. "Lots of people want to ride with you in the limo, but what you want is someone who will take the bus with you when the limo breaks down" (Unknown).

Relationships in Business

When you first start a business venture with a partner or family member, you usually do not have much but dreams and hope for the future. This means that both of you are usually on the same page, but as the business begins to grow, money starts to come in, and you each have personal changes in your lives, the dynamics of that relationship will change. Things will happen that put you both in tough situations. One of you may get married or have a child, and now that you have additional family responsibilities, you can no longer commit as much time to the business.

On another note, there may be one who feels like the other is getting more recognition than the other. At this point competition begins to set in as to who gets their picture on the front page of the newspaper, who gets to do the news interview, and whose house is the largest. Many of these are trivial, but they are just enough to make the foundation of the business crumble and with it the customer base, the family, and the initial relationship that started the business in the first place.

Another thing that often happens is the family members start to intervene with the running of the business. The spouse of one of the partners may start to say things like "You always do all the work and never get any vacation, so when are we going to spend some quality time alone?" At this point, the dynamics are changing, and so is the business structure. There is also the scenario in which one of the partners is stealing from the business or abusing company resources. What do you do?

Legally the other person is as much a part of the business as you are, and perhaps he or she can justify why he or she used the company credit card to buy furniture for his or her home. Though the rationale may be weak and very much unjustified, it is still the rationale. Now you are stuck with a dilemma that you have no idea how to get out of. You are furious and cannot believe that your trust has been violated, and in the back of your mind you want to choke your partner.

The best thing to do is take a deep breath, communicate with your partner, and then work through your attorneys if all else fails. Again, remember this little theory, and life will be much better: *The only people you need to get even with are those who have helped you.*

Relationships are truly the key of life. Whether a business relationship, a spiritual relationship, or a physical relationship, they all should be approached with caution. Great relationships make all the troubles of the world seem small or at least manageable, but bad relationships can make life simply intolerable, and what at first seemed like a small problem can often end up a huge mess, leaving one to wonder how they got there in the first place.

Many people want to have strong relationships, but they do not demonstrate the skills to cultivate them. If you want to foster some good relationships, treat people as if they are old friends. Be excited to see them, or at least show them that their presence means something to you. Make them feel at home.

Who knows; your ideas combined with their resources may lead to the next major business deal, but if you were rude at the first encounter or came across as standoffish, then you are assured not to gain any ground. Many feel that if they extend themselves, they are making themselves vulnerable. This is true but only to an extent, because by treating people kindly you give up some power, but in turn you can gain much more. I am not saying that you put all your trust in them and completely open up, but from a distance you can be cordial and come across as a concerned friend.

Everyone wants to feel special, even if they act as if they do not. Give them a chance to prove you wrong about them. Never extend more than you can afford to lose. That way if they do betray you, you do not lose much, but you learn so much about them and can slowly move away from the relationship.

You do not have to decide who is acting and who is genuine, because if you treat everyone as old friends you will begin to form good relationships regardless of their intentions. If the relationship is not meant to be then it won't be, and all it will cost you is a few smiles and a little time, but the time was worth it to find out who the person really was before you introduced them to your family, started loaning money to them, formed a business with them, or began telling them your most cherished secrets.

Marriage and Spiritual Relationships

One very serious relationship is marriage. Marriage is a relationship that needs to be approached as one of the biggest business transactions that you will ever make. People often look at marriage for all the bliss and peacefulness that they always imagined it would be, but it can be quite the opposite. Plus, if it doesn't work out, like so many of them do not, it can be quite costly both financially and emotionally. Marriage is a tough process, because it puts limitations on people, and it also asks that each person make strong commitments to the other. These are commitments that many are not truly up to.

When marriage is carried out effectively, it can be beautiful because two individuals are coming together for common goals. This can be debt consolidation, constant companionship, and raising children. However, when things are not so well, it can become a matter of who can hurt who the most and who can gain the most out of the failed relationship. There is a price to pay for imperfect information, and though you may never know all things about a person, it is important to do as much research as possible. We are looking into these types of relationships because we need to have the knowledge. Knowledge is power, and power is the ability to determine outcome. We are talking about these relationships because it can be a very costly mistake to marry the wrong person. Just ask some of these Hollywood celebrities who thought marriage was a game. They now know the truth.

The spiritual relationship just might be the toughest of them all to expound upon. This is because it is much more individually faith-based than scientifically proven. Many feel that there is definitely a higher power that rules the world and that this higher power can change your destiny at any point in time. I will not tell you what you should believe, but know that you should believe in something.

I believe in the value of relationships, but I am cautious when dealing with man. Man has the ability to earn your faith but then just as soon lose it. How many times have we seen some pastor, judge, doctor, teacher, or entertainer who has abused their privileges? Whether that is to physically abuse a member of the congregation, mistreat a patient, hand down a sentence that is unjust, or touch a young child in an inappropriate manner, it happens on a daily basis, in many locations across the globe.

I am very seldom surprised to see the injustices that are committed by man no matter what his or her title. I have come to the realization that no matter your title, you are still a human, and because of this, you are susceptible to human nature. You are susceptible to the temptations and ills of the world. I see many people who get so caught up in their job, their school, or their church that they often lose the ability to think rationally. That is fine; do what you think is best, but in my opinion, you have to judge right and wrong based on the actions of the world, not just faith alone.

The people who are praying for me on Sunday may just be the same ones cussing me out on Wednesday. This is the world we live in, and if you are to be successful, then you should know the types of individuals who may cross your path every day, and then determine how that relationship affects your life. When I see a teacher who has abused a child, a coworker who has done something inappropriate, a comedian who repeatedly uses racial slurs, or a minister who has taken advantage of a parishioner, I may be the only one in America who is not surprised. I put no man on a pedestal, but I do show respect for those who build up others' lives, and I pray for those who tear them down.

The question for you is what is your reaction when you learn of this type of betrayal? It is very easy to turn the other cheek, and write the offense off when it is just another news story, but true leaders find a way to hold everyone accountable for their actions, and no one gets a pass. Not the professional athlete, not the movie star, not the CEO. At some point you will have to answer for your actions, as karma is real, but this may be something that you have to take up with the creator, as nothing truly goes unseen.

The spiritual relationship is one that you will have to decipher for yourself, but I can tell you that you will often need to have faith to keep going. You must realize that faith alone only gets you to the door, and at some point you will have to take some action to open it. Faith will often make things possible, but it does not necessarily make them any easier to accomplish. I pray to God that after reading this you will achieve all the levels of success that you so desire, and I have the faith that you will do just that, but at the end of the day, you will have to take appropriate action to achieve your success, or my prayers will have just been in vain.

We have discussed a lot in this chapter, but just remember that there is power in relationships, both good and bad, and for you to be successful, it pays to have strong relationships; it pays to have a strong network. Your NetWork equals your Net-Worth!

EIGHT

Education Is the Key

Out of all the key ingredients you will need to succeed, none of them will have as much effect on your life as education. *I often say that education is what you get when you read the fine print, and experience is what you get when you don't.* There is no way for me to emphasize how important it is to train and educate your mind. It is that one gift to yourself that will keep on giving as long as you live. In every situation your education will be the foundation from where you can begin, and if education is not the foundation, be weary. As now you are not making decisions based on your knowledge, you will be making them based on assumptions or based on someone else's thoughts.

Many say that the United States is the only place where *education is mandatory, but learning is optional.* I feel that this is a slap in the face to our educational system. "The National Center for Education Statistics notes that in October 2000, more than 10 percent of America's young adults were not enrolled in high school or had not completed it."[6] The United States has long been the front runner in areas such as business, politics, and economics, so to fall behind in education is just not acceptable. The United States had become the flagship of what others viewed as successful, but somewhere along the line we seem to have gotten off track. "The United States is falling when it comes to international education rankings, as recent studies show that other nations in the developed world have more effective education systems. In a 2003 study conducted by UNICEF that took the averages from five different international education studies, the researchers ranked the United States No. 18 out of 24 nations in terms of the relative effectiveness of its educational system".[7]

Many reasons have been cited as to why many schools do not have good test scores or why many high school teens drop out. Many will say it's because there were no parents in the home to ensure that the child learned the importance of education. Others will say it is because of overcrowding in the

---

6   http://nces.ed.gov/pubs2002/droppub_2001, Dropout rates in the United States: 2000, National Center for Education Statistics.

7   http://kapio.kcc.hawaii.edu/upload/fullnews.php?id=52, Wu, Elaine, "U.S. falls in education rank compared to other countries," The Kapio Newspress, 2004.

classrooms. Some others will say they are trying to make a difference, but they are not allowed to because the school board has their hands tied as far as what and how the curriculum should be taught. These are all very valid excuses, but they are not good enough for those who want to be successful and want to see others succeed.

The successful individual understands that behind all of these excuses are students who are destined to fail. For every excuse a teacher is forced to make, that's possibly one more child whose chances for success are diminishing. If we want a nation of people to be successful, we must find a way around all barriers to education. If we truly want to breed a populace of prepared minds, or if we all want to be successful ourselves, then we must find a way around all educational barriers.

There are cities that build new football stadiums for upwards of $150 million, but when a teacher complains of overcrowding, or lack of resources, they are often told the budget is blown, and their complaints often fall on deaf ears. This says to me that we have misappropriated the funds and compromised our priorities.

It also says to me that we need to write to our local congresspeople and have them take action immediately. If the school board is not allowing our teachers and principals to do their jobs, then we need to congregate at the front of the school board and at the front of city hall to have our voices heard. If we do not, then we have possibly failed every kid that came into our classroom, did not obtain the knowledge, and is sent on to the next grade. For every child that makes it to the tenth grade and cannot read, every person they have come in contact with up to that point has failed them.

Many times a student does not achieve in school because they do not see the value in it, so they do not apply themselves and end up missing a lot of the lessons, but they often do see the value of sports and other extracurricular activities. This tells me we have to make learning more appealing. A wise man once said that to appeal to the masses we must first learn to appeal to the interests versus the intellect. This is why most people can name two American Idol champions but not the two senators that represent their state.

The Problem of Priorities

We need to get our priorities straight with academics coming before sports, because this glamour of professional sports is overshadowing the apparent boredom of obtaining an education. Perhaps those who make our laws and decisions are such sports fans that they could care less if a child graduates from high school. As a country we seem to be sending the wrong message. Let's think about this for a second: if athletes made $40,000 a year and teachers made millions, would we then get our kids to become students again? Or how much would the sports industry change if before you could play professional sports you had to earn a college degree? Would this change the mindset of our student athletes, or would colleges lower standards so that these athletes could pass and entertain us on the playing field? These are hypothetical questions, but questions that should be asked.

I enjoy sports as much as many, and I do not feel these athletes are overpaid, seeing that this is what the fans demand, but if it means that a nation of students won't learn their lessons at the expense of playing professional sports, I say get rid of sports and let's educate future minds. This may be drastic and farfetched, as sports help children learn how to work as a team as well as develop other traits such as confidence and discipline, but my point is that education should come before everything else. In my speeches I say *it must be Education before PlayStation.*

On top of this, these teachers need to be paid more for what they are called to do, and I am a champion for paying the athletes a little less if it means getting the teachers more. If this compromise cannot be made, and sometime soon, then perhaps we should all start to boycott the arenas where these games are played and the vendors and companies that sell their products there. I'm saying do not buy a single hot dog, fountain drink, bottled water, jersey, or anything else until we take care of the ones who educate our kids. With that type of drastic action, I bet education will start to take priority again, just as it should.

As soon as we stop accepting excuses, that's when we can begin implementing the solutions that will make our students and ourselves successful. There is no shortcut when it comes to education, and do not let anyone tell you otherwise. No matter what you want to achieve in life, it pays to be educated. Knowledge is power, and power is the ability to determine outcome. Do not let others fool you into thinking that even money will cure the problems of an uneducated mind. We discussed earlier that money is not the key to success, and neither should you think that it is an alternative to obtaining an education. The way I see it, if you give ten million dollars to a thug, you have just made him a ten-million-dollar thug, you have not enhanced his mental capacity, you have not made him a rational thinker, and you have not made him socially conscious, so do not be surprised if he goes out and blows the money on cars, clothes, or jewelry.

A well-known quarterback in my city is suffering from some poor choices that he made. Though he has millions of dollars, the choices he has made have left him vulnerable to many, in and outside the sports world, who are now coming after his millions and his reputation. I cannot help but feel that a stronger educational base would have assisted him in making some wiser decisions. What he could not see before is now becoming more and more clear everyday.

The Value of Education

My attempt is to get you to buy into this process long before the negatives potentially take over your life. I am serious about this education chapter and want you to know that there are many who do not share my thoughts. They feel that education is a waste and that they can do without it, seeing they expect to be professional athletes, entertainers, and entrepreneurs. Granted, obtaining an education and acquiring knowledge takes work; it's a never-ending process.

It can also be an expensive process, especially once you get into the ranks of college and post-college, but as the saying goes, *"education is expensive, but ignorance costs so much more."* I can tell you that even highly paid individuals benefit from having an education. Education is the foundation that will prepare you for lifelong decision making. We will all make some poor choices over the course of our lives. Many of us will make mistakes simply because we chose to do something that we knew may not be in our best interest, while others will make mistakes because they did not have the knowledge base to make a better decision, and some will make mistakes because due to where they are in life, they may see no other option but the wrong one.

As stated earlier, a lack of optimism often comes from what is viewed as a lack of options. Your education will afford you those additional options. There will be many reasons why a person may not be able to further his or her education, but I do not feel there are many valid ones. Perhaps there were years ago when children helped work the land or worked to earn money to support the family, but in today's society I can think of very few reasons to forego your education.

If you have not prepared yourself during the early years, then pursuing an education is not an attractive alternative, because you may not have the base needed to continue. This just means seventh grade algebra may be extremely tough for you if you did not learn fourth grade multiplication. You will most likely spend all day hoping the teacher does not call on you instead of attempting to learn. It is our responsibility that the children of tomorrow understand and grasp their education. Many talk about not leaving any children behind, but they are leaving them behind every day, and if you are like me, this should be a wake-up call that we must change the policies and procedures to obtain better results.

With a lot more businesses moving overseas and outsourcing more jobs, it is becoming even more difficult to earn a decent living in the U.S. The good jobs are becoming even more challenging to find and tougher to obtain. With this being said, it pays to be educated. It pays to be viewed as an asset to a company, and if you are starting your own company, then it pays to be educated for that as well. Education will only help to ensure the success of your enterprise.

From kindergarten through the completion of high school, your number one priority should be your books. Also starting in kindergarten should be the planning process of what is to come after the completion of high school. There should be no discussion of anything less than earning a high school diploma. The teachers should make this a point in daily conversations. There should also be further discussion and promotion of the idea of college and how it will be paid for. The earlier a person can plan for their education, the more of an advantage they will have going through the process and the more likely it is that they will go on to complete their college studies.

I would view anything less than this as failure, and you know that is not what this book is about. This book is about becoming successful, and with that I am giving you direct steps to gain this success versus allowing you to give up and then bet on the exception. If I wanted you to bet on the exception I would have told you on the first page to forget your education and just go buy a lottery ticket.

Many will argue that a college degree is a waste of time and that it is not needed. Do not listen to these individuals, as they are trying to bet on the exception. College is a tool that will act as a security blanket should any other plans go awry. It does not guarantee you success but will heighten your chances. *It will never hurt you to have a college degree.*

I have heard many say that their children are not college material. My question to them is at what point did they say it was okay for their children to give up? In the event your child wanted to drop out of school in the seventh grade, would you then have said that your child was not seventh grade material? No, you would not have, so do not allow excuses when it comes to the success of your children. I am not saying that those without high school diplomas or college degrees are not or cannot be successful, because they can, but the odds are much higher that they will not. I am simply saying that by having a sound education you are preparing yourself for greatness that may often elude you without it.

Success consists of going from failure to failure without loss of enthusiasm.

— Winston Churchill

NINE

Get Excited; It's Your Only Option

Success is the most exciting phenomenon in the world. Nothing gives a person more enjoyment than succeeding in a process that means a lot to them. This may be the process of birthing a child, playing a full round of golf under par, or climbing the corporate ladder to Senior VP status. It's the success that makes all the trials and tribulations that much sweeter.

Success is truly the only option; just ask the right people. If you ever get a chance to speak with Oprah Winfrey, Michael Jordan, or Bill Gates, ask them what makes them successful. They will probably have an easy time responding to this, simply because they only know one way to be successful and that is to be the best.

It is important to understand that your road to success started many years ago with your ancestors, who began paving the way for themselves. As a result of their lineage, work ethic, and ability to transfer their skills, you have been the beneficiary of many things that happened long before you were ever in the equation. Many times the ability to solve problems, work with your hands, or play sports is in your genes. If you can believe this, then you should also believe that you were born with many of the tools you need to be successful, but that does not mean you will be. Just possessing a hammer and nails does not mean the picture will ever hang on the wall. You still must do the work in order to be successful.

You must understand what the word success means to you before you can plan your course of action. Remember, success may come in many forms, depending on your situation. There was an author on the television a few weeks ago, and he described wealth as a word stemming from the word well-being. He says that you have to look at how life's events affect you emotionally, physically, spiritually, and financially. There are so many people who have sold their souls to make more money, or they have compromised family members so they could prosper in other areas. These individuals did not realize that had they just held on a little longer, their success was coming regardless, without putting their friends and families in harm's way.

When it comes to success, an individual's potential is often just as important as his experience. During speaking engagements I often hear people attempt to earn credibility by telling me how many years they worked in corporate America. My question to them is always, "What was your role, and in what departments did you work?" What I find most of the time is that the person worked thirty years for the same company in a concentrated area such as the finance department.

This is a very important area of the company, especially if the person was a decision maker in the organization, but more times than not, the person had a standard role for two years or so before going to a similar role within the same department. After fourteen or so position changes, the person knows 110 percent about their role but only 20 percent about their company. The roles they had only gave them one viewpoint, and though they were on the job thirty years, they did not get to see how operations worked, how human resources worked, and what is done on the shipping and receiving docks. The person has become a specialist in one area, and if I ask him or her whether I should place $100,000 in their company stock and why, he or she cannot give me the reasons why the company is a good buy.

The fact is that he or she does not have enough information. Here again we say that the potential is often equal to or greater than the actual experience, and even better than that is when we combine the potential with experience.

Another question I get as a speaker is, "You do not even look twenty-five years old; what can you teach us about leadership, motivation, or success, when most of us in this room have been working longer than you have been walking?" At this point, I ask the audience these basic questions.

Twenty years ago, who was your cell phone carrier? Twenty years ago, what Internet provider were you using? Twenty years ago, what was your favorite DVD? Twenty years ago, were you able to ship a package to Mainland China overnight? The fact is that twenty years ago, none of these things were an option for you. Life and business have both changed over the past twenty years. Do not get me wrong; this is not to make light of anyone's years of service, as they are priceless, but seeing that my potential for greatness is high, perhaps we need to combine your contacts, wisdom, and financial resources with my youth, energy, and potential to be successful.

Life has changed so much in the past twenty years, and though your experience is irreplaceable, the age of technology has virtually re-pioneered the way we do business, and for those who do not want to change, their chances of success are rapidly diminishing. Do any of you remember individuals who swore never to use the computer because they never needed it in the past, or simply because they were unfamiliar with it, causing them fear? They are probably the same ones who are still trying to buy cassette tapes, VCR tapes, and typewriter ribbon. Technology has made it possible for those who have the desire to succeed at a much faster rate, to do so while cutting out half the steps that it took twenty years ago.

Successful people tend to possess the same traits. These can be but are not limited to: Competitiveness, Confidence, Resilience, Empathy, Optimism, Persuasiveness, Perseverance, Creativity, Courage, Desire to Learn, Willingness to Take Risks, and a Strong Desire to Win!

Focus on the Positive; File Away the Negative

One that is not on this list but I feel the need to add is selective amnesia. Successful people have a strange way of remembering things. They seem to have a file in their minds that remembers all the good things. Anything bad they log in the back of their minds, and they only recall it when it is needed for their success. They tend not to focus on the negatives but find a way to concentrate on the positives they have experienced. These are the things that will always put a smile back on their faces even when they are down.

I remember once when I was on vacation in Pompano Beach, Florida. I had been one of the top basketball talents in that area during my high school days. There was a park where all the ball-players would go to test their skills. Well, now that I was back in town, as my family had moved to Chicago years previously, my friends and I decided to play some pickup basketball.

I felt like this was just too good to be true. It was 88 degrees in Florida versus 28 degrees in Chicago. I was back on the court with a number of my friends, and my skills had gotten sharper, as a couple years had passed since I last played with the guys. To top it all off, my girlfriend at the time was sitting on the sideline with all the other beautiful girls who always came out to watch us put on a show.

As the game got going, my buddy Dreamer and I got into our zones. We always played well together due to my speed and ball-handling ability and his size and ability to shoot. As the game became intense, the trash talking began, coming from both sides of the court. Dreamer and I were running plays as if we had been playing together for years, and every time we did something spectacular, we heard the girls laugh and giggle. There was one guy on the other team who was tall, broad-shouldered, and talked a lot of trash, even though he was not good. The game was just about over, and Dreamer and I said we were going to go right at him.

The very next play, I grabbed a rebound and ran down the court at top speed, and sent a no-look pass cross court to Dreamer, who caught the ball in mid-stride, and like an airplane defying the wind, lifted off. With arms and legs flying everywhere, the only person who tried to jump up and block Dreamer's shot was the loudmouth from the other side. I'll never forget that picture of Dreamer hanging in the air and then twisting his body so that he could get to the rim. As Dreamer extended his arms and reached over the opponent, he slammed the ball down with a mighty force.

The opponent fell backward onto the blacktop pavement, where one of his shoes came untied and the other completely fell off his foot, as if a bolt of lightning had hit him. The blast from the dunk had knocked the sole completely off the shoe that had come off, and when we saw the sole it was rolling and flapping down the court as if someone was still walking in it. It was one of the funniest sights you ever wanted to see.

We all laughed at what had just transpired and had to suspend the game for about ten minutes, just to regain composure and honor on the court, as all the girls and guys were hysterical at what just happened. Though embarrassed, the guy whose shoes had come off, put his shoes back on and resumed playing. I ran into him about a year or so after the incident, and I asked if he remembered that day. Of course his answer was, "No, that was not me," and of course I said, "Oh, yes, it was."

I put that image in my mental Rolodex and can see it as if it happened yesterday. Just like I remembered, I am positive that he did too, but since it was an embarrassing negative experience for him, he had tucked it far away in the back of his mind. Successful people somehow find ways to draw strength from the good times and tuck away the bad ones.

They find a conscious way to remember the good things and an unconscious tendency to channel out the negatives, only drawing on those negative experiences when they are needed. Even though he told me that he did not remember, I bet he will instinctively know what to do next time when a six-foot-four, 225-pound state champion basketball player comes at him. You see, that day is in his personal folder, but it is not one that he will draw up often. Only when the experience is needed to aid in his success will he reflect on the negatives.

Now that is a funny but true story, and whether it is sports, business, music, or academics, you too will need to be able to file away the important experiences and recall them as needed. This is what I call selective amnesia, in which we choose to remember what we want to remember. I can remember all the report cards on which I got straight A's, which was not many, but I do not recall many I got when my grades had fallen. The moral is that by remembering the good things, I can always continue to shoot for greatness rather than get bogged down in the negatives, which will often discourage and diminish your desire to keep going.

Look for Opportunities Other Than the Obvious

To be successful you have to look for the opportunities that are not often seen and perhaps do not even exist. Many times you will have to create the opportunity and then make others see why they need your product or service. You do this by advertising, writing letters, and making phone calls. You have to create a buzz around whatever it is that you are promoting, and if you do not believe in it, why should anyone else?

This is not always easy to do. I hear people who are trying to break into the music industry complain about how they have to compete with the larger acts for radio airtime. Then they say it is impossible to compete with these larger acts that have more to spend on promotion. I say nothing is impossible until you think it is. Sure, the major acts have larger advertising budgets, but to me that does not mean they have more to spend; that means they have more to lose. This is how successful people view obstacles, and you should do the same. Find the reasons why you can win, and don't make excuses why you cannot.

The Wisdom of Listening

To be successful we must learn to listen. Many times we get so caught up in a person's looks, what they drive, or where they live that we often hear what we want to hear. We end up not listening at all but hearing what our eyes are telling us. Take a person who is blind and responsible for all of their day-to-day actions. They often have listening skills that are out of this world, and by utilizing these skills, they visualize things through sound that you and I may never encounter even through sight.

It is amazing to watch those who are without sight but full of direction. They can cook and clean for themselves, take the subway to work, and give you directions to locations that they have never seen. To these individuals, your looks, your car, and your house mean nothing. They are listening to your words and following your actions to determine your credibility and willingness to succeed.

The fact that they do not have sight does not mean that they do not have vision. In fact, they use their other skills to see far beyond their means. As they do not have the power of sight, their eyes do not cloud their judgment when it comes to decisions, certain biases, and having to purchase the flashiest suit on the rack. Listening is a great tool that most of us do not do particularly well and the person who stands up to argue this is further proving the point that we are so defensive and so ready to speak that listening goes right out the window. If you want success, practice improving your listening skills, listen for understanding, listen for opportunities, and last of all, listen to become better.

The Power of the Brain

We also must do a better job of sharpening our minds. The brain is the most lethal tool you have in the hunt for success, so do not abuse it. Say no to drugs and alcohol, and if you are of legal drinking age and must drink, limit the amount you intake. All of these external ingredients work to prevent the mind from functioning to its full potential, which in the end limits your capabilities.

Use your mind. Even with all the computers, calculators, and BlackBerrys here to assist you, there are times when no source is better than your own memory. Once you become so dependent on these electronic tools, you will begin to doubt what your mind tells you, and at that point you have no choice but to lean on the decision-making power of others or these popular gadgets. "All recent theories in mind development agree that, like the universe, there is no known limit to one's memory."[8] "The law of entropy basically states that if we don't use it, we lose it. Unless we continually exercise our brain by feeding it information through learning, our ability to retain information deteriorates."[9]

Use your mind to make wise decisions, decisions that will help you achieve your objectives. As stated earlier, I hear people say they are going to drop out of college, and they can point to numerous people who are successful without furthering their education. My answer once again is that these people are betting on the exceptions. *Do not bet on the exceptions, because they are just that, exceptional.* It's a lot like the lottery: they show you the one person who has won the million dollars, but they never show you the thousands of people who have lost.

Many people talk about Bill Gates not finishing college, which is true. Bill dropped out of college when he did not feel that college was his thing, but understand that Bill was not just a regular person. In fact, the school he dropped out of was Harvard. Just the simple fact that this future computer mogul was enrolled at Harvard should tell you that he was not your average student.

---

8   Bennett, Bo, "Year to Success," Archieboy Holdings, LLC, 2004 -2006, 35.

9   Bennett, Bo, "Year to Success," Archieboy Holdings, LLC, 2004 -2006, 452.

Make decisions that will allow you to reach your goals and maximize your potential. Bill Gates is definitely an exception. He is one of the world's richest men, and there are only a few of those, but if you educate your mind, surround yourself with good people, and make wise decisions, no one is saying that you cannot make the Forbes list of the wealthiest individuals as well.

Success is that fuel that keeps us striving for more. It is a concept and life practice that makes each individual do things that under normal conditions we probably wouldn't do. None of us want to be normal, and because of this we try harder to improve our positions in life. We attempt to make our lives better. Success consists of setting out on a mission and then accomplishing that mission despite all obstacles and challenges that we may face.

Once reached, the bar for success must be adjusted so you can continue to challenge yourself and in turn put an extension on your greatness. You cannot expect exceptional results by doing normal things. In office meetings, the definition of insanity is doing the same thing over and over, the exact same way, and expecting different results. You must analyze the process, find out what you can do differently, and make the appropriate changes in an effort to manifest your dreams.

CONCLUSION

As we look back, let's look at from where we have come. We now know that life is not fair, so we should not expect it to be. We must continue to find ways to overcome challenges, and then reach for our success.

We also must realize that everyone has talent, but is it true talent, or is it a gift? We must learn the difference, and then display our talents to the world in an inconspicuous way. We must find a way to toot our own horn.

It takes work to become successful; it does not just come to you. You must believe in your success and put forth the effort to achieve it. One way to make your journey easier is to create the perception that you are the best for business, the subject matter expert, and the best for overall profitability.

Always remember the formula that we worked out in Chapter Four, which said that attitude equals

100 percent. No matter the situation, try to keep a positive attitude, and things will work themselves out. The difference between a bad event and a catastrophe is always your attitude. Always remember everyone loves a winner, so remain positive.

What will you do to get over the bar? What will you do when 100 percent is just not good enough? What will be your motivation to keep reaching for greatness? On top of this, do you realize how important politics is to your company or community?

True leadership is something you will have to determine for yourself. Perhaps we are living in an era where leadership is promoted, but what people really want to see is great followers. Do not get lost in the shuffle; continue to demonstrate why you should be up front. Leadership is not what you do to me; it's what you do with me.

Never forget how important relationships are to your success. Most of the things we want to accomplish in life will require the assistance of someone else, so remember to treat individuals as old friends. This way you are always increasing your network. Your network equals your net worth!

Education is the key. No matter what you want to accomplish in life, it helps to be educated. They say we live in a country where education is mandatory and learning is optional. Do not let anyone tell you that your education is not valid or valuable. It is the one gift that will keep on giving. Despite all the debates you may have heard, it never hurts to have a college degree.

Chapter Nine says for you to get excited about your success, as it's your only option. Success is truly the only option for those who choose to be successful. They will not stop until they have accomplished their goals. Success can be found at the intersection where preparation and opportunity meet, so prepare yourself, and when the opportunity presents itself you will be ready to seize it. You are working toward success in your life, the only life you will ever have.

Now that you have read this book, you are prepared with the tools that you need to succeed in life. The key is to succeed, not simply survive. Just like success will make individuals do things that they normally wouldn't do, so will survival. Know the difference between the two, as one is used for greatness, and the other is used to simply get by.

Wake up every day with a purpose, a mission, and a reason to be great. This is your life to win, and no one has the right to enjoy it as much as you. So prepare yourself, work hard at being the best, and become a "go-getter." Do not just wait for things to come your way — make them come your way. "Success usually comes to those who are too busy to be looking for it" (Henry David Thoreau).

Just as reading this book will change your life,

writing it has changed mine. I am able to see visions of greatness for you. I can see future leaders taking the torch and running with it as well as average ideas becoming dynamic examples of what ideas plus effort and commitment can do. I hope that you have enjoyed this book as much as I have enjoyed writing it.

It is now time for you to take action. It is time for you to claim your success. Take the next few days and write your goals and objectives on a piece of paper. Next, make all of these goals time-based, and commit that you will stick to the schedule. If you do these things, you will find success somewhere along the way. This book cannot personally ensure your success, because that will be determined by how you apply yourself and the tools needed to become successful, but if you stick to the program and tell yourself that you will not quit until you win, then success will be your reward.

By doing this, you will be holding yourself accountable for your actions, and at that point you will start to win; you will begin to become successful. I believe that you are the best; I believe that you are a winner; I believe that you will become successful. The question is, do you believe in yourself? Just remember that success is your only option; just ask the right people. And with that being said, you now know *How to Make It in a World That Wasn't Made for You*!

ABOUT THE AUTHOR

Larry H. Jemison Jr.

Larry Jemison is a powerful consultant, author, and motivational speaker. He is president of The Jemison Group, LLC, based just outside of Atlanta, Georgia, where the primary focus is "to enhance your social and business acumen, which ensures that success becomes your only option." Larry earned a master's degree in business from Babson College, which is often noted as the number-one program in America for Entrepreneurial Studies (*U.S. News & World Report*).

Prior to this, Larry earned a marketing degree from Tuskegee University, where he graduated with honors from the esteemed historic institution that produced the likes of Tom Joyner, Lionel Richie, and the Tuskegee Airmen. He is a member of the Atlanta Urban League Young Professionals, member of the National Sales Network, founder of the Atlanta Dream Makers Networking Group, and a member of the Hotlanta Hackers Golf Club. He has spent over twelve years in the corporate sector as a leader in the areas of finance, training, and marketing and sales with companies such as FedEx, Novartis Pharmaceuticals, and Lucent Technologies.

You may have seen Larry yourself in motion pictures such as *The Fighting Temptations*, starring Cuba Gooding Jr. and Beyonce Knowles, and *Motives*, starring Shemar Moore and Vivica Fox. He has also done multiple commercials for The Weather Channel and been interviewed on XM Satellite Radio's *Warren Ballentine Show*, as well as V103's *Frank Ski Morning Show*. The Georgia Secretary of State recently honored Larry for his role in supporting prostate cancer awareness.

How to Make It in a World that Wasn't Made for You is his first book. You can learn more about Larry or book him for speaking engagements at www.larryspeaks.com.